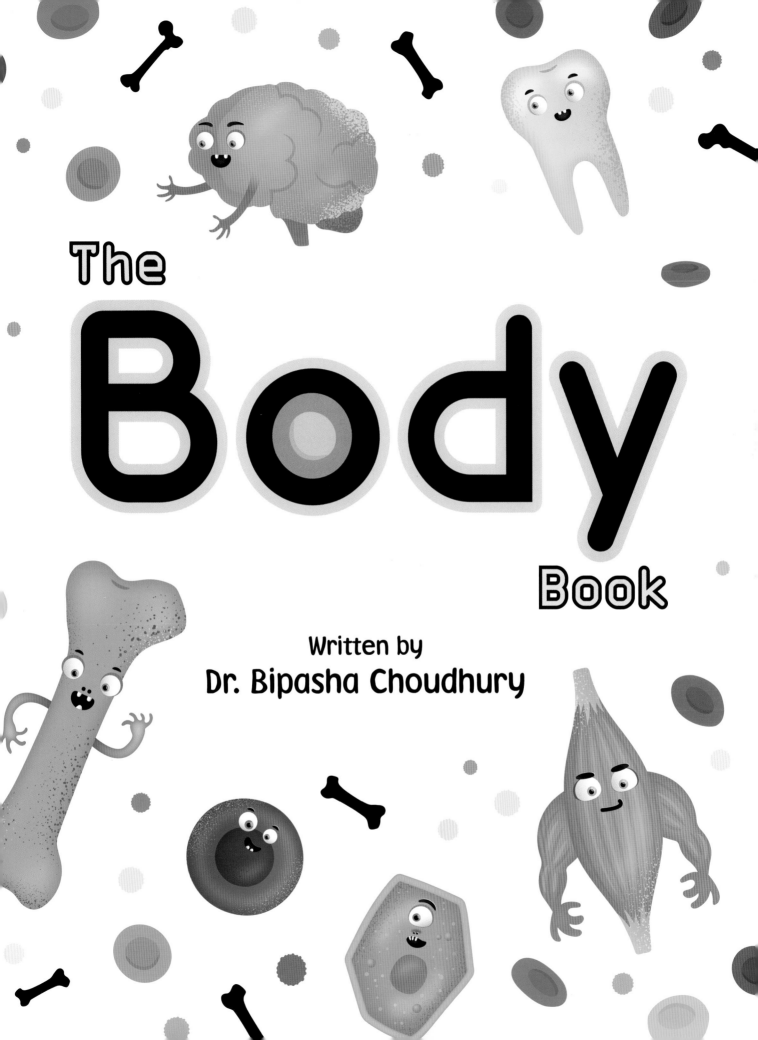

The Body Book

Written by
Dr. Bipasha Choudhury

Contents

DK | Penguin Random House

Written by Dr. Bipasha Choudhury
Consultant Dr. Kristina Routh

Project editor Manisha Majithia
Designer Bettina Myklebust Stovne
Illustrators Mark Clifton,
Bettina Myklebust Stovne
Additional editorial Olivia Stanford,
Katie Lawrence, Kat Teece,
Sally Beets, Kieran Jones

Additional design Elaine Hewson,
Karen Hood, Lucy Sims
Jacket coordinator Issy Walsh
US editor Mindy Fichter
US senior editor Shannon Beatty
Jacket designer Karen Hood
Senior production editor Nikoleta Parasaki
Senior production controller Isabell Schart
Managing editor Jonathan Melmoth
Managing art editor Diane Peyton Jones
Deputy art director Mabel Chan
Publishing director Sarah Larter

First American Edition, 2022
Published in the United States by DK Publishing
1450 Broadway, Suite 801, New York, NY 10018

There are some **tricky words** relating to the body in this book! Check the **glossary** if you come across any you're not sure about.

Published in Great Britain by Dorling Kindersley Limited
A catalog record for this book
is available from the Library of Congress.
ISBN 978-0-7440-5022-6

DK books are available at special discounts when purchased in bulk for sales promotions, premiums, fundraising, or educational use. For details, contact: DK Publishing Special Markets, 1450 Broadway, Suite 801, New York, NY 10018
SpecialSales@dk.com

Printed and bound in China

For the curious
www.dk.com

MIX
Paper from responsible sources
FSC™ C018179

This book was made with Forest Stewardship Council ™ certified paper – one small step in DK's commitment to a sustainable future. For more information go to www.dk.com/our-green-pledge

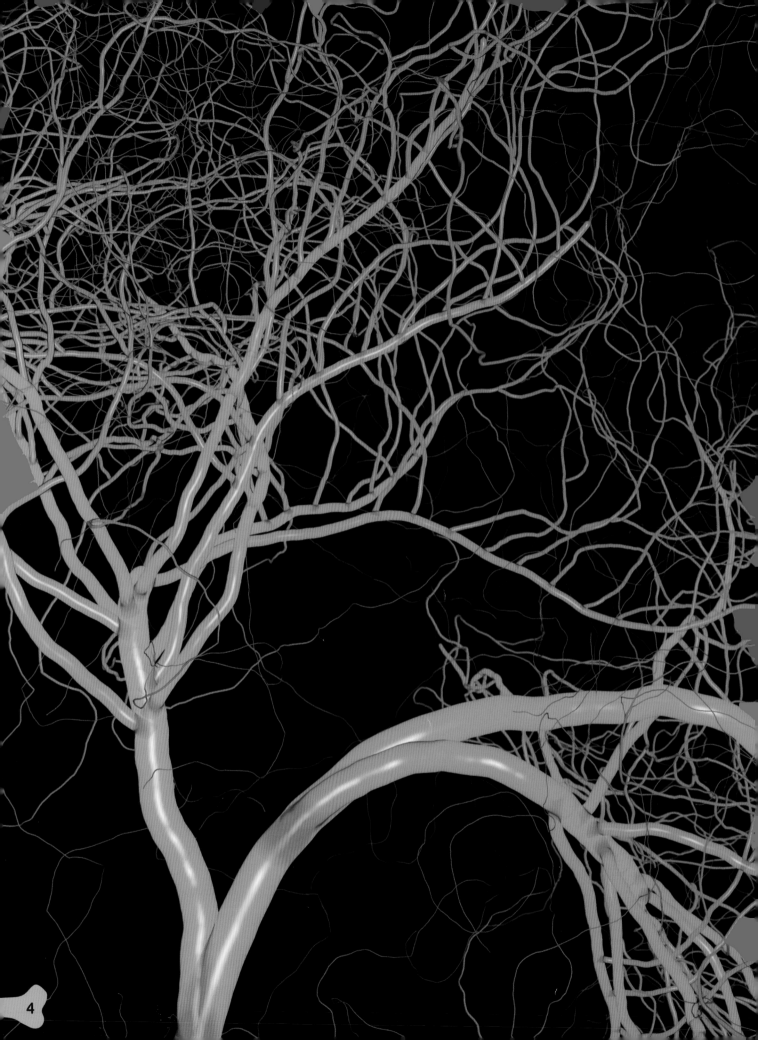

4

Introduction

Your body is simply amazing! It carries out countless different activities each day, such as walking, eating, and thinking—and many more without you even realizing it. Do you ever wonder why you don't forget to breathe? Or how many times your heart needs to pump each minute? Your body does this all for you on its own! All the **body's organs work together**, a little bit like an orchestra, to keep every part of you going strong.

In this book, we'll take a closer look at the **inner workings of the human body**, and you'll discover how our understanding of the body has changed since ancient times. I hope you will come to appreciate just how **unique and wonderful** your body is!

Dr. Bip Choudhury

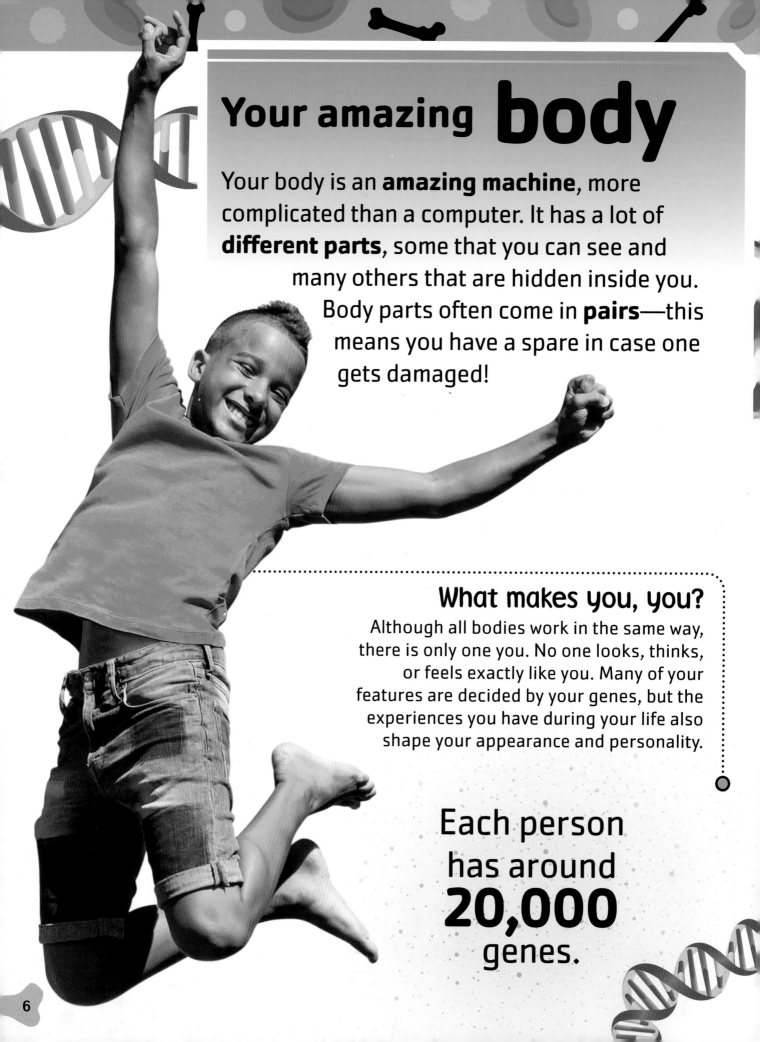

Your amazing **body**

Your body is an **amazing machine**, more complicated than a computer. It has a lot of **different parts**, some that you can see and many others that are hidden inside you. Body parts often come in **pairs**—this means you have a spare in case one gets damaged!

What makes you, you?

Although all bodies work in the same way, there is only one you. No one looks, thinks, or feels exactly like you. Many of your features are decided by your genes, but the experiences you have during your life also shape your appearance and personality.

Each person has around **20,000** genes.

Genes

Each of your body's cells contains genes—a set of instructions that builds every part of you. You have two versions of each gene, one from your mother and one from your father. Your genes are unique to you, but twins that look the same share most of their genes.

Chromosomes
There are 23 pairs of chromosomes in each cell. Half are from your mother and half from your father.

Nucleus
This is the instruction center of a cell. Your chromosomes, which contain your genes, are found every cell with a nucleus.

DNA
Chromosomes are made of tightly coiled strands of a chemical called DNA. When unwound, DNA looks like a twisted ladder.

Genes
Sections of DNA are called genes. There are thousands of genes in each chromosome.

Genetics

Children look like their parents because of the genes they inherit from them. You inherit some genes from one parent and some from the other parent. This is why you might have eyes like your mother's but hair the same color as your father's.

This child has inherited brown eyes from her father.

Groups of organs form organ systems. The mouth, throat, stomach, and intestines make up the digestive system, which takes energy and nutrients from the food you eat.

ORGAN SYSTEM

ORGANISM

Inside out

Together, all the organ systems make one complete organism. Each part of the body, from a cell to a system, has to function properly to keep us healthy.

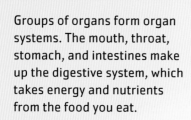

ORGAN

Organs are composed of two or more tissues that work together to carry out a particular function. The stomach lining works with muscle tissue to digest food.

Bone is a type of **connective** tissue—it connects different body parts.

TISSUE

A lot of cells that do similar jobs combine to form tissues. The cells here are from the lining of the stomach and their job is to produce stomach acid.

TYPES OF CELLS

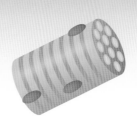

Red blood cell
These cells have no nucleus and are a special shape so they can fit through vessels.

White blood cell
There are different types of white blood cells. They fight off infections.

Fat cell
Fat cells are found throughout the body and are an important store of energy.

Muscle cell
These cells make up muscles that contract and relax to help you move.

Nerve cell
Nerve cells send electrical messages around the body to tell it what to do.

What are we made of?

The smallest building block of the body is the **cell**. Groups of cells make **tissues**, which combine to make **organs**. All the organs put together form an organism, like you!

CELL

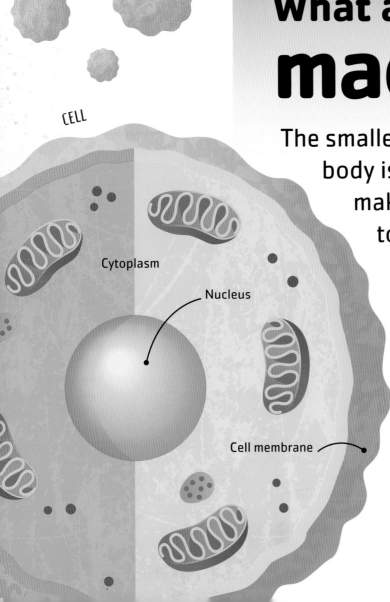

Cytoplasm

Nucleus

Cell membrane

Cells are held together by a skin, called a membrane. Inside is a soup-like liquid called cytoplasm in which organelles, or "mini organs," float around. The most important organelle is the nucleus—it contains instructions that tell the cell what to do.

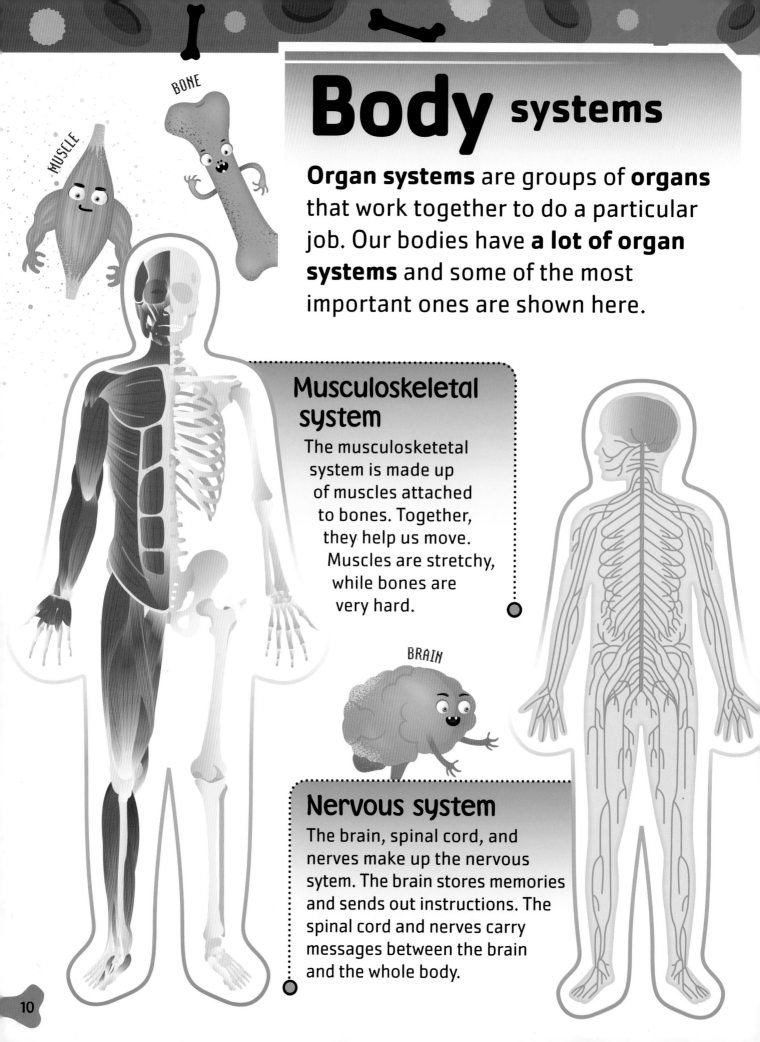

MUSCLE

BONE

Body systems

Organ systems are groups of **organs** that work together to do a particular job. Our bodies have **a lot of organ systems** and some of the most important ones are shown here.

Musculoskeletal system

The musculosketetal system is made up of muscles attached to bones. Together, they help us move. Muscles are stretchy, while bones are very hard.

BRAIN

Nervous system

The brain, spinal cord, and nerves make up the nervous sytem. The brain stores memories and sends out instructions. The spinal cord and nerves carry messages between the brain and the whole body.

Respiratory system

This system is made up of the lungs and airways. It helps us breathe in air full of oxygen and gets rid of the waste gas carbon dioxide.

Other body systems

There are several more organ systems not shown here. These include the renal system, which makes urine, and the immune system, which fights infections.

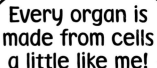

Every organ is made from cells a little like me!

SKIN CELL

RED BLOOD CELL

TOOTH

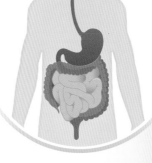

Cardiovascular system

The cardiovascular system is made up of the heart and blood vessels. One of its main functions is to supply all parts of the body with oxygen, which is carried by red blood cells.

Digestive system

This system starts at the mouth and ends at the anus. Its job is to digest food so that the body has plenty of energy. Strong teeth start the process by breaking down food.

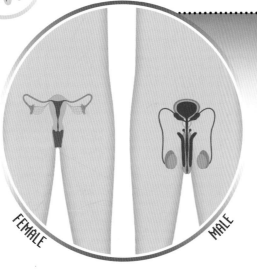

FEMALE

MALE

Reproductive system

Babies wouldn't be born without this system. Male reproductive organs make sperm, and female organs make eggs. These join together inside the woman's uterus, where the baby grows.

Your super
skeleton

Your skeleton acts as **a frame** for your body—it keeps everything together and your muscles attach to it. The bones in your skeleton are **strong** and some **protect** your organs.

BALL-AND-SOCKET JOINT

Joints

A joint is formed where two or more bones meet. The bones are held together by tough tissues called ligaments. Joints let us bend, stretch, and dance! A joint that can move in almost any direction, such as the hip joint, looks like a ball in a socket.

The **funny bone** is not a bone at all— it's a **nerve** behind

Cartilage

CARTILAGE

A flexible tissue called cartilage is found where bones meet, protecting their surface to stop it from wearing away. Your ears and the front of your nose are also made of cartilage. That is why they feel a little bendable.

X-RAYS

X-ray images help doctors to see if bones are healthy. The "X" in X-ray stands for "unknown" because X-rays were discovered by accident!

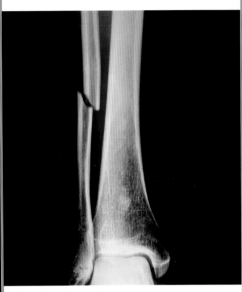

Broken bones
Bones are so dense, or solid, that they appear white on an X-ray image. Can you spot the broken bone in this X-ray?

Inside the bone

The outside of a bone is hard, but the inside is soft, spongy, and full of holes—this makes it light. Bones are filled with a jelly-like substance called bone marrow, and the holes contain many blood vessels and nerves.

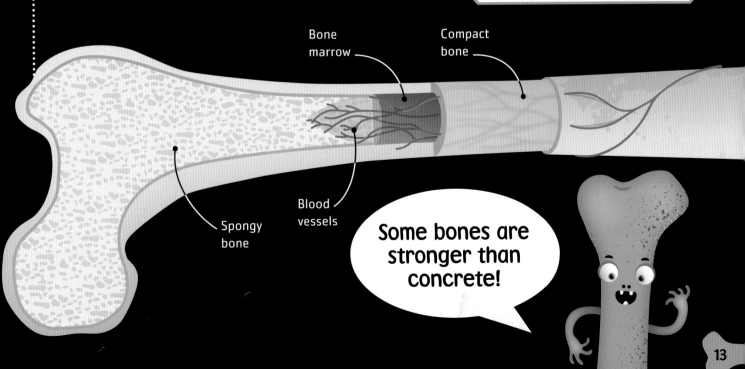

Bone marrow

Compact bone

Spongy bone

Blood vessels

Some bones are stronger than concrete!

Working in pairs

Muscles work together in pairs each time you move. For example, the biceps muscle works with the triceps to help bend and straighten your arm when bowling.

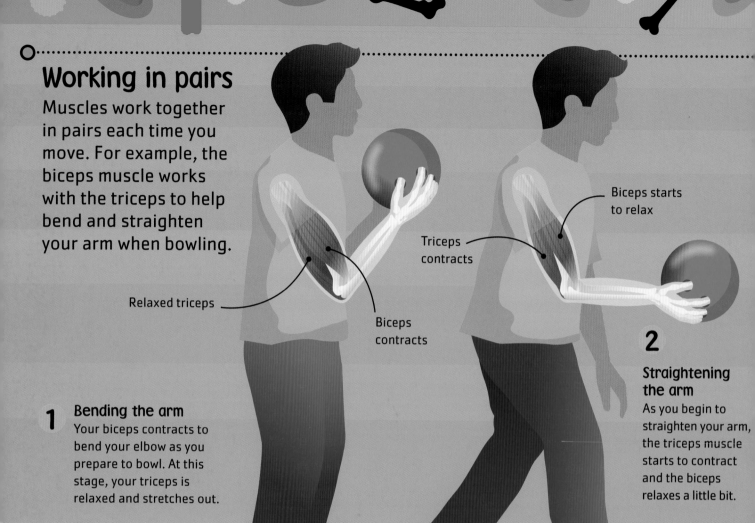

Relaxed triceps

Triceps contracts

Biceps starts to relax

Biceps contracts

1 **Bending the arm**
Your biceps contracts to bend your elbow as you prepare to bowl. At this stage, your triceps is relaxed and stretches out.

2

Straightening the arm
As you begin to straighten your arm, the triceps muscle starts to contract and the biceps relaxes a little bit.

Mighty **muscles**

Anytime you **move** your body, groups of muscles work together to make movement possible. When one muscle **contracts**, or pulls, the other muscle **relaxes**. Muscles let you walk, smile, and blink!

The largest muscle in your body, the gluteus maximus, is in your butt.

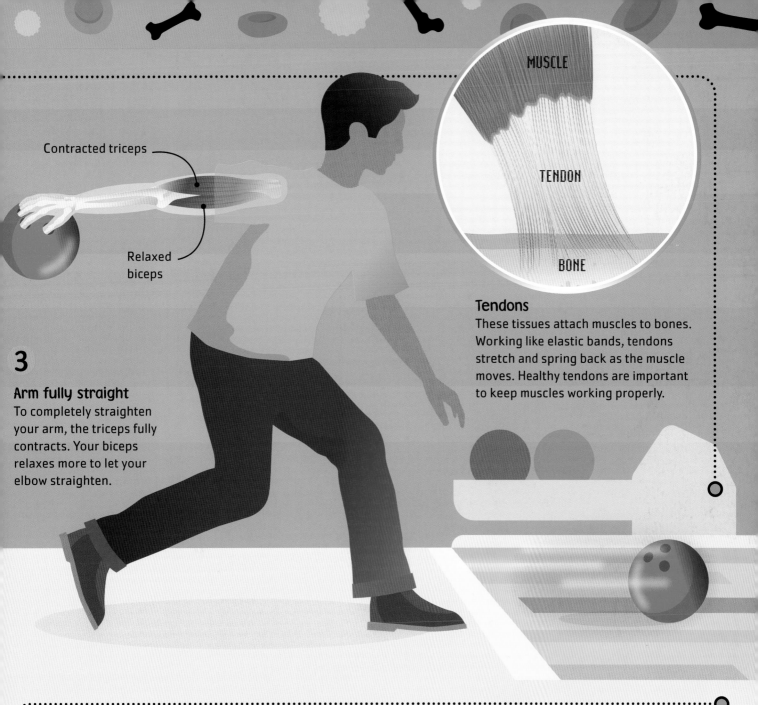

Contracted triceps

Relaxed biceps

MUSCLE

TENDON

BONE

Tendons
These tissues attach muscles to bones. Working like elastic bands, tendons stretch and spring back as the muscle moves. Healthy tendons are important to keep muscles working properly.

3
Arm fully straight
To completely straighten your arm, the triceps fully contracts. Your biceps relaxes more to let your elbow straighten.

Types of muscles
Different types of muscles are needed in different places in the body. Skeletal muscles move when we want them to, but cardiac and smooth muscles work continuously on their own.

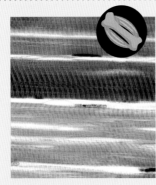

Skeletal
Attached to the skeleton, these muscles pull on bones to make them move.

Cardiac
The heart is made of cardiac muscle, which keeps it beating to pump blood around the body.

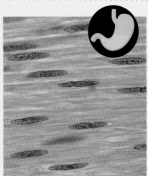

Smooth
Smooth muscle is found in the walls of organs, such as the bladder and the stomach.

The beating heart

Your heart is a **bag of muscle** that pumps blood around the body. Blood flows through its **four chambers**: two atria and two ventricles. Veins carry blood to the heart, and arteries carry blood from the heart to the body.

The pulmonary arteries carry oxygen-poor blood to the lungs.

Lungs
Your lungs and heart work together to deliver oxygen to, and remove carbon dioxide from, the body.

Blood supply

The heart needs its own blood supply to work. Coronary arteries carry oxygen to the heart wall, and coronary veins take away waste products, such as carbon dioxide.

Heart
Heart chambers keep oxygen-rich and oxygen-poor blood separate.

The pulmonary veins carry oxygen-rich blood from the lungs to the heart.

Closed valve
Blood stops flowing

Open valve
Blood flows freely

« VALVE TRANSPLANTS

Heart valves keep blood flowing in the right direction. Sometimes, they stop working properly. If this happens, artificial heart valves can be inserted into the body. The first heart valve transplant was performed in the 1960s.

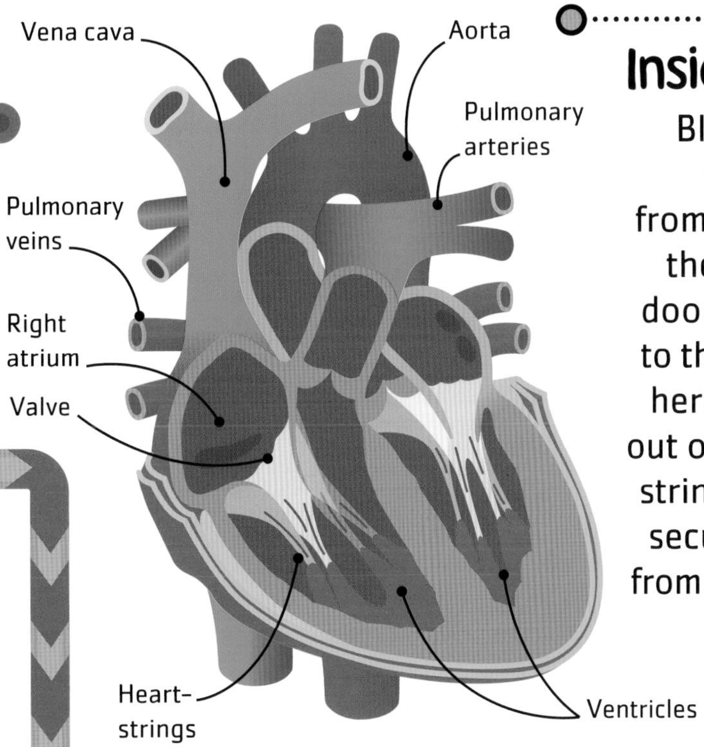

Vena cava

Aorta

Pulmonary arteries

Pulmonary veins

Right atrium

Valve

Heart-strings

Ventricles

Inside the heart

Blood flows into the left and right atria from the whole body. It then passes through door-like valves to get to the ventricles. From here, blood is pushed out of the heart. Heart-strings keep the valves secure, and stop them from turning inside out!

The aorta, the biggest artery in the body, delivers blood to the body.

Around the body
Your heart beats non-stop to keep blood flowing to all parts of your body, even when you are sleeping!

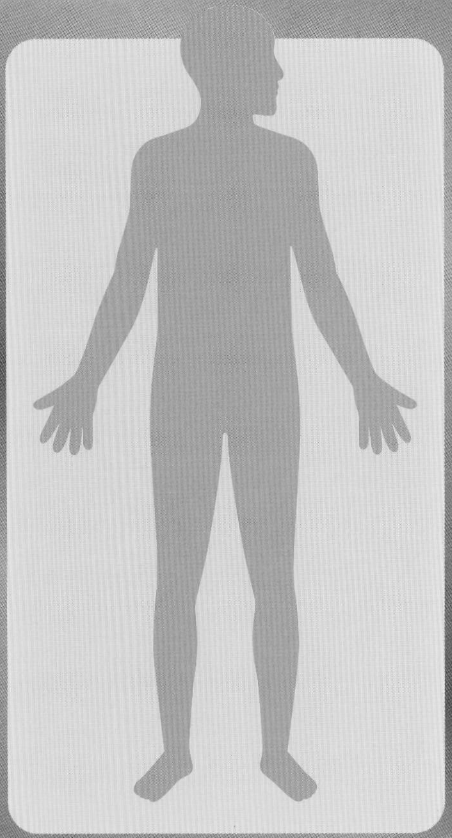

Your heart beats between 70 and 120 times per minute!

The largest vein in the body, the vena cava, carries oxygen-poor blood from the body to the heart. The blood contains carbon dioxide, a waste gas.

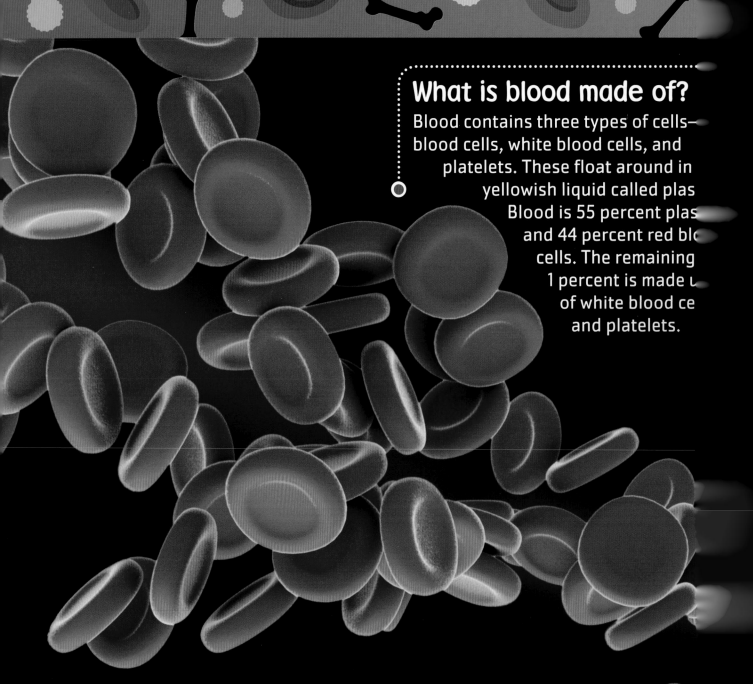

What is blood made of?

Blood contains three types of cells— blood cells, white blood cells, and platelets. These float around in yellowish liquid called plas Blood is 55 percent plas and 44 percent red blc cells. The remaining 1 percent is made u of white blood ce and platelets.

Blood

Blood travels to every part of your body through a network of tubes called **blood vessels**. It delivers **oxygen** to the body to keep it working, and removes **carbon dioxide** by carrying it to the lungs to be breathed out. Blood also **fights infections**.

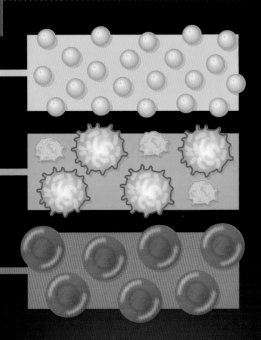

Plasma

Plasma is mostly made of water. The rest is a mix of substances, including antibodies—which fight infections—as well as protein and waste matter.

White blood cells and platelets

White blood cells patrol the body to kill germs. Platelets, found in plasma, help to heal cuts and wounds.

Red blood cells

Red blood cells contain a protein called hemoglobin, which carries oxygen. Hemoglobin also gives blood its red color.

Some **animals**, such as crabs and lobsters, have **blue blood**!

BLOOD TYPES

There are four main blood groups: A, B, O, and AB. The antigen, or protein, on the red blood cell determines which type you are.

Type A
The A antigen lives on the surface of the red blood cell.

Type B
The B antigen lives on the surface of the red blood cell.

Type AB
Both A and B antigens are found on the cell's surface.

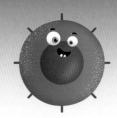

Type O
There are no antigens on the cell's surface.

The story of **blood**

People's knowledge of **blood** and **how it circulates** around the body has changed greatly since ancient times. Over the years, careful **study of the human body** has helped our understanding of how blood works.

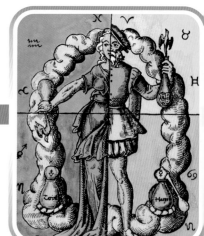

Ancient Egyptians
In Ancient Egypt, it was believed that different vessels carried fluids, such as blood, snot, and tears, from organs in the body to the heart.

Four humors
Ancient Greek doctors believed the body had four "humors": blood, phlegm, black bile, and yellow bile.

Knowing the different blood groups made blood transfusions much safer.

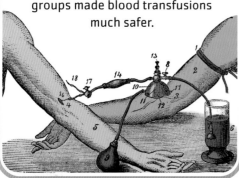

A transfusion is when blood is transferred from one animal to another.

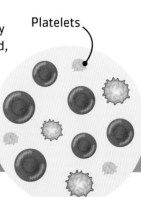

Blood groups
The different blood groups were discovered by Austrian scientist Karl Landsteiner in 1901.

Blood transfusions
Scientists successfully carried out blood transfusions in dogs and sheep before the first successful human–to–human blood transfusion in 1818.

White blood cells
In 1843, white particles were seen in blood along with red ones— this was the discovery of white blood cells.

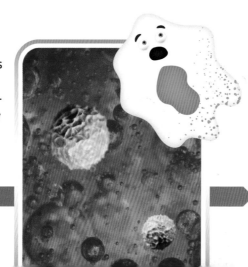

Platelets
Scientists had seen oddly shaped granules in blood, which they had thought were damaged blood cells. In 1882, it was discovered that they were in fact platelets.

Platelets

Ancient India

Around 600 BCE, Indian doctors believed that by feeling the pulse, they could tell if the humors were balanced correctly.

TOUCH YOUR WRIST TO FEEL BLOOD PUMPING.

Blood makes up around **8 percent** of your body weight.

IN 1678, RED BLOOD CELLS WERE SEEN UNDER THE MICROSCOPE FOR THE FIRST TIME.

Blood vessels

Ancient Romans were the first to suggest that blood was carried in blood vessels. However, they also thought that the liver made blood, and from there it flowed to the body.

William Harvey

This British doctor discovered the connection between the heart and blood vessels, and showed how blood was transported to and from the rest of the body.

Plugging blood

At the start of the 20th century, experiments showed that platelets in blood flock to the site of an injury, creating a blood clot to stop the bleeding.

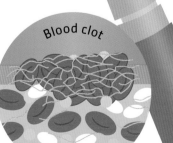

Blood clot

Today

When blood is donated today, the white blood cells are removed. The red blood cells and platelets may be separated so they can be used where needed.

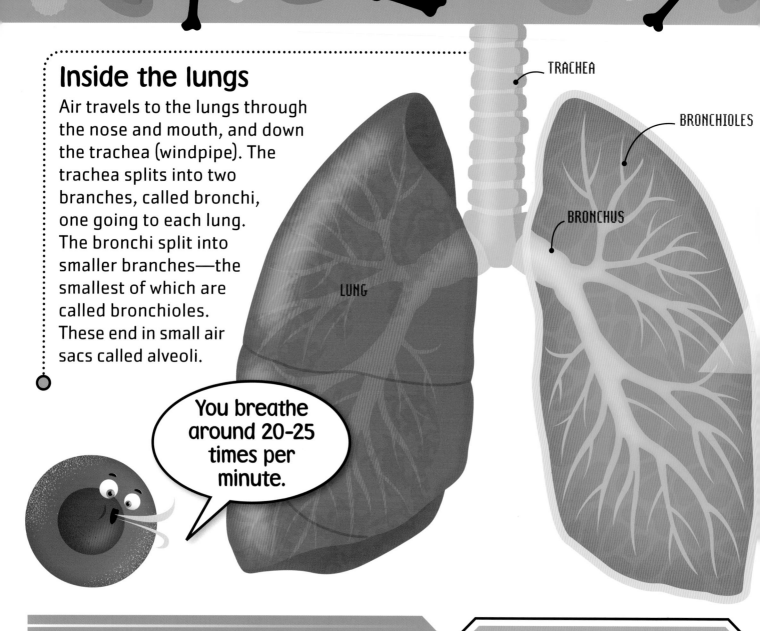

Inside the lungs

Air travels to the lungs through the nose and mouth, and down the trachea (windpipe). The trachea splits into two branches, called bronchi, one going to each lung. The bronchi split into smaller branches—the smallest of which are called bronchioles. These end in small air sacs called alveoli.

TRACHEA

BRONCHIOLES

BRONCHUS

LUNG

You breathe around 20-25 times per minute.

Breathe in

When you breathe in, your lungs fill with fresh **oxygen** gas, which is needed to make your body's cells work. **Carbon dioxide**, a waste gas, is removed from your body when you breathe out.

« A HELPING HAND

The "iron lung" was a machine used to help people with breathing difficulties. The patient laid inside a large metal tube, and air was pumped in and out to keep their lungs working.

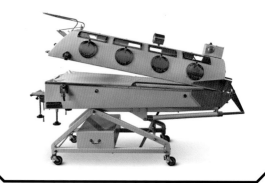

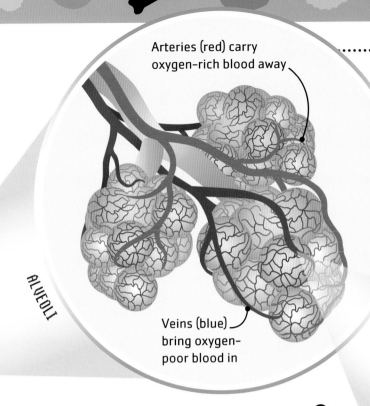

Arteries (red) carry oxygen-rich blood away

ALVEOLI

Veins (blue) bring oxygen-poor blood in

Exchanging gases

A lot of tiny blood vessels called capillaries wrap around each alveolus, allowing the gases to move in and out. Oxygen passes through the walls of the alveoli into the blood, whilst carbon dioxide moves into the alveoli to be breathed out.

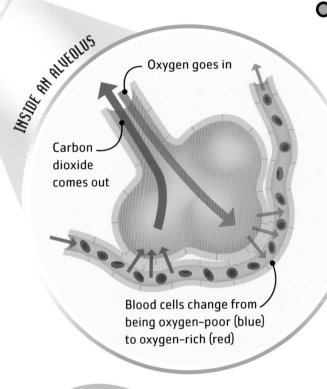

INSIDE AN ALVEOLUS

Oxygen goes in

Carbon dioxide comes out

Blood cells change from being oxygen-poor (blue) to oxygen-rich (red)

In and out

The diaphragm is a large sheet of muscle under your ribcage. It contracts and relaxes when you breathe to pull air into your lungs and push it out. Muscles attached to the ribcage move it up and out when you breathe in, to fit your expanding lungs.

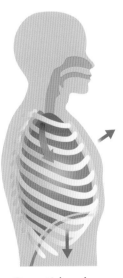
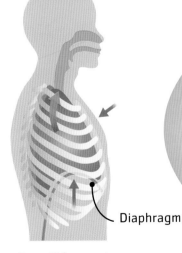

Diaphragm

Breathing in
The diaphragm flattens, and the lungs and ribcage become larger.

Breathing out
The lungs and ribcage shrink, and the diaphragm relaxes upward.

Your lungs are like balloons that **inflate** when you breathe in and **deflate** when you breathe out.

Your brilliant **brain**

Everything you see, hear, do, feel, and think is **controlled** by different parts of your brain. It contains billions of cells, called **neurons**, that communicate with the rest of the body through a large network of nerves.

Cerebrum
The largest part of the brain is the cerebrum. Its outer layer is split into four different "lobes."

FRONTAL LOBE

EMOTION

Personality
The frontal lobe is home to your personality. This affects how you behave, and what you like and dislike.

MOVEMENT

Moving
The commands that tell your muscles what to do come from the frontal lobe.

SOUND

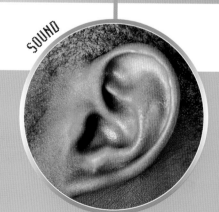

Hearing
The temporal lobe makes sense of the sounds picked up by the ears. It helps you to hear and talk.

Awareness
External information, such as temperature, pain, and pressure, are sent to the parietal lobe. This makes you more aware of your surroundings.

ENVIRONMENT

SIGHT

Seeing
Everything the eye sees is sent as signals to the occipital lobe. It then processes the information to form an image.

MAP OF THE BRAIN

PARIETAL LOBE

CEREBRUM

TEMPORAL LOBE

OCCIPITAL LOBE

CEREBELLUM

BRAIN STEM

One-fifth
of your blood supply goes to the brain.

Cerebellum
The cerebellum helps the muscles of your body work together to make smooth movements.

LEFT AND RIGHT SIDE
The cerebrum is made up of two halves, called hemispheres. The left hemisphere tells the right side of the body what to do and the right hemisphere tells the left side of the body what to do.

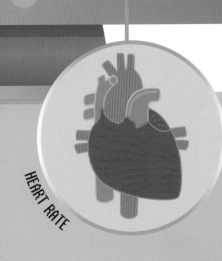

HEART RATE

Control center
Just under the cerebellum is the brain stem. It joins the brain to the spinal cord and controls important functions, such as breathing and heart rate.

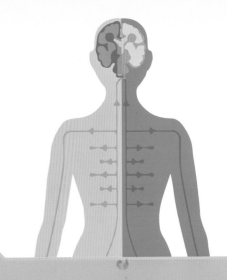

Network of **nerves**

Every part of the body needs a **nerve supply** in order to work properly. Nerves are like electrical wires, **carrying information** in the form of signals all around the body. The **nervous system** controls everything you do.

Neurons

Nerves are made up of bundles of cells called neurons. Electrical signals travel along the neuron's length—from the dendrites to the nucleus, and then along the axon. A chemical is released at the synapse, passing the signal onto the next neuron.

Your brain has around **86 billion** neurons!

Axon
The electrical impulse travels down the axon, a long, thread-like fiber, to the end of the neuron.

Myelin sheath
Many axons have a protective covering, which helps information travel faster.

Nucleus
The nucleus is found in the cell body. It controls the neuron.

Spinal cord
This large bundle of nerve tissues links the brain to the rest of the body. Signals travel from nerves in the body along the spinal cord to the brain, where the information is processed.

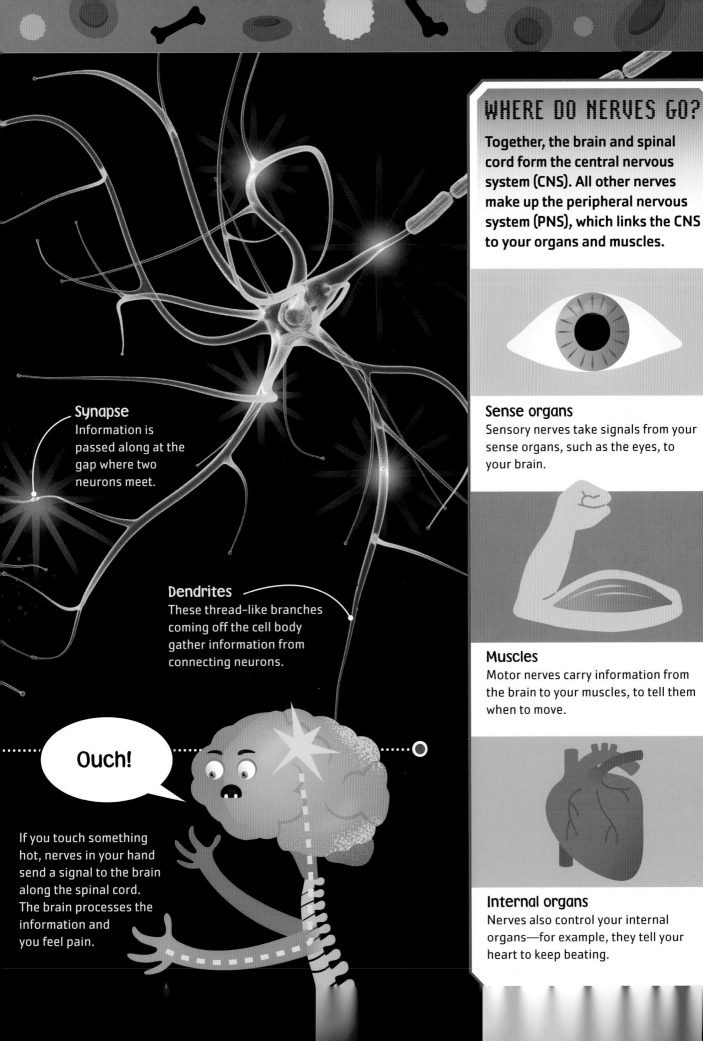

Synapse
Information is passed along at the gap where two neurons meet.

Dendrites
These thread-like branches coming off the cell body gather information from connecting neurons.

Ouch!

If you touch something hot, nerves in your hand send a signal to the brain along the spinal cord. The brain processes the information and you feel pain.

WHERE DO NERVES GO?

Together, the brain and spinal cord form the central nervous system (CNS). All other nerves make up the peripheral nervous system (PNS), which links the CNS to your organs and muscles.

Sense organs
Sensory nerves take signals from your sense organs, such as the eyes, to your brain.

Muscles
Motor nerves carry information from the brain to your muscles, to tell them when to move.

Internal organs
Nerves also control your internal organs—for example, they tell your heart to keep beating.

The secrets of skin

Skin is the **largest organ** in the body. It keeps your body wrapped up and **protects your insides**. **Sensory receptors** in the skin detect what is going on around you and **keep you safe** from danger.

> Skin cells only live for 30 days.

Under the skin

Skin is made up of two layers. The thin outer layer is the epidermis. Below this is the dermis, a thick layer full of nerves, blood vessels, and glands.

Pores
Tiny holes on the skin allow sweat to leave the body.

Epidermis
This layer is waterproof to keep you dry. The epidermis grows new skin cells every month.

Blood vessels
These get bigger when the body is too warm, allowing heat to escape from the blood through the skin.

Dermis
Elastic fibers located here make the skin stretchy.

Sweat glands
These glands make salty sweat to help cool you down.

Hair follicle
New hairs grow from tubes called hair follicles.

Nerves
These send signals from receptors to the brain.

◀◀ LEECHES

Leeches are worms that have been used in medicine since the late 1700s. They suck on blood and release substances that numb the skin, stop blood clotting, and make blood vessels get bigger. Fresh blood then flows to the skin, helping it heal.

AMAZING SKIN

Skin tones

Skin contains a chemical called melanin—the more melanin you have, the darker your skin is. Sometimes, your skin makes extra melanin in the sun to protect you from its harmful rays. This is why you get a suntan.

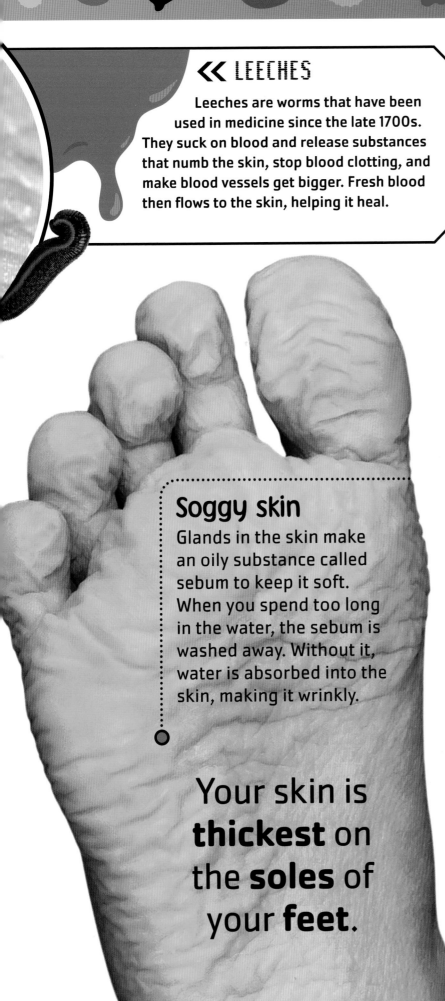

Soggy skin

Glands in the skin make an oily substance called sebum to keep it soft. When you spend too long in the water, the sebum is washed away. Without it, water is absorbed into the skin, making it wrinkly.

Your skin is **thickest** on the **soles** of your **feet**.

Healing

Tiny cells in the skin called fibroblasts help to heal cuts and wounds. They arrive at the injury and start to make new skin. This includes scar tissue, which is 80 percent as strong as the original skin.

Growing old

As we age, our skin becomes less elastic. We produce fewer elastic fibers and less sebum, and we also lose water from our bodies. This makes skin stiffer and wrinkly.

Nails

Nail keratin is clear. Nails look pinkish because of the blood vessels that lie underneath them. Try pressing down on a fingernail and see how it turns white—this is because you've blocked the tiny blood vessels!

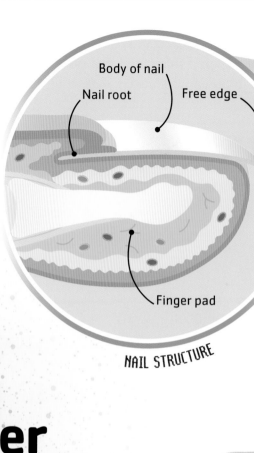

Body of nail

Nail root

Free edge

Finger pad

NAIL STRUCTURE

Fingernails grow **four times faster** than toenails!

Nails and hair

Made of a strong protein called **keratin**, hair and nails help to **protect your body**. Keratin cells are dead, which is why it doesn't hurt when you cut your hair or nails! The **roots** are the only parts that are alive.

Scalp hairs
These protect the head from becoming too hot or too cold, and from objects that might cause injury.

Eyelashes
These delicate hairs stop dust and other objects from entering and damaging the eyes.

Hair

Hair strands grow out of tiny holes called follicles. The part of the hair you can see is the shaft, and the root is below the skin. Each hair follicle is surrounded by nerves—that's why it hurts when you pull hair out! Oily glands near the follicle keep the hair healthy.

HAIR SHAFT

Plates of overlapping keratin make up each hair strand.

Brrrrr!

GOOSEBUMPS

Under your skin, attached to the base of your hair follicles, are tiny muscles called arrector pili. When you feel cold, excited, or scared, they contract to make the hairs on your arms stand up straight. The skin looks a little like a goose without feathers!

Vellus hairs
These very fine hairs cover most of the body and help to keep us warm.

Types of touch

The skin contains different types of receptors, which allow you to feel different things. Most are found in the dermis, the skin's lower layer, but the receptors for heat, cold, and pain reach out to the top layer of skin, called the epidermis.

Temperature

Thermoreceptors detect temperature. They protect you from extreme temperatures, sending signals to your brain if something is too hot or cold.

There are more than **3,000** receptors in each of your fingertips!

Light touch

These receptors are found all over in the skin, especially in the fingertips, and areas with body hair. This is how you can tell when a feather tickles you.

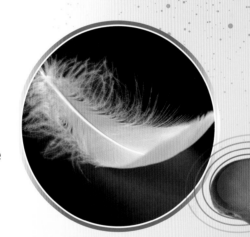

Touch

The **skin** is full of sensors, called **receptors**, which give you your sense of touch. They allow you to **feel what's around you**, so that you can respond—for example, by protecting yourself from harm.

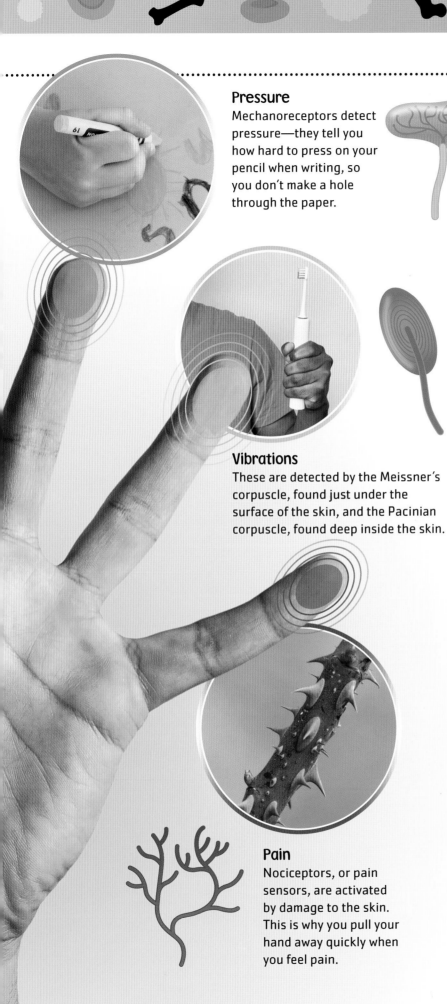

Pressure

Mechanoreceptors detect pressure—they tell you how hard to press on your pencil when writing, so you don't make a hole through the paper.

Vibrations

These are detected by the Meissner's corpuscle, found just under the surface of the skin, and the Pacinian corpuscle, found deep inside the skin.

Pain

Nociceptors, or pain sensors, are activated by damage to the skin. This is why you pull your hand away quickly when you feel pain.

How sensitive?

This image is known as a sensory homunculus, in which the body parts with the most receptors are largest and those with the least are smallest. This shows that the hands, fingertips, and lips are especially sensitive.

READING WITH TOUCH

Braille is an alphabet that can be read using touch. Each letter is represented by a pattern of raised dots, which can be felt by the fingertips to figure out words.

Eyes and sight

Your **eyes** are responsible for your sense of sight, allowing you to see what is going on around you. They **collect light** from objects and process the information to **create images** of what you are looking at.

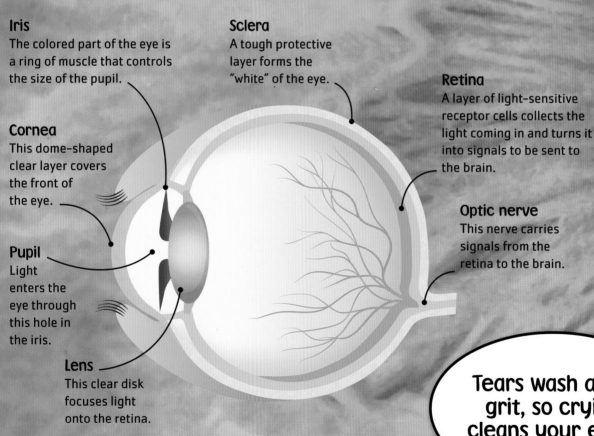

Iris
The colored part of the eye is a ring of muscle that controls the size of the pupil.

Cornea
This dome-shaped clear layer covers the front of the eye.

Pupil
Light enters the eye through this hole in the iris.

Lens
This clear disk focuses light onto the retina.

Sclera
A tough protective layer forms the "white" of the eye.

Retina
A layer of light-sensitive receptor cells collects the light coming in and turns it into signals to be sent to the brain.

Optic nerve
This nerve carries signals from the retina to the brain.

Inside the eye

Light enters the eye through the pupil. The light is focused onto the retina at the back of the eye and the information is sent to the brain. The pupil changes in size based on the lighting conditions. It gets bigger in dim light and smaller in bright light.

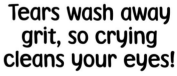

Tears wash away grit, so crying cleans your eyes!

Just like your **fingerprint**, your **iris** is **completely unique** to you!

SEEING IN 3D

Look straight ahead and notice how much you can see without turning your head. This is your visual field— it is really large! This is because both eyes pick up light separately and send slightly different signals to the brain. The brain combines the signals to create a single 3D image of what you are looking at.

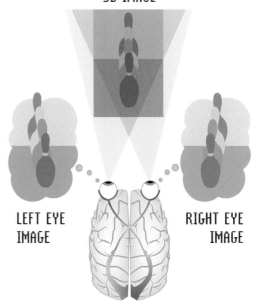

3D IMAGE

LEFT EYE
IMAGE

RIGHT EYE
IMAGE

Eye muscles

Six tiny muscles move the eyeballs in different directions. They work together to make sure the movements are smooth. If one of the muscles doesn't work properly, it can result in blurred vision.

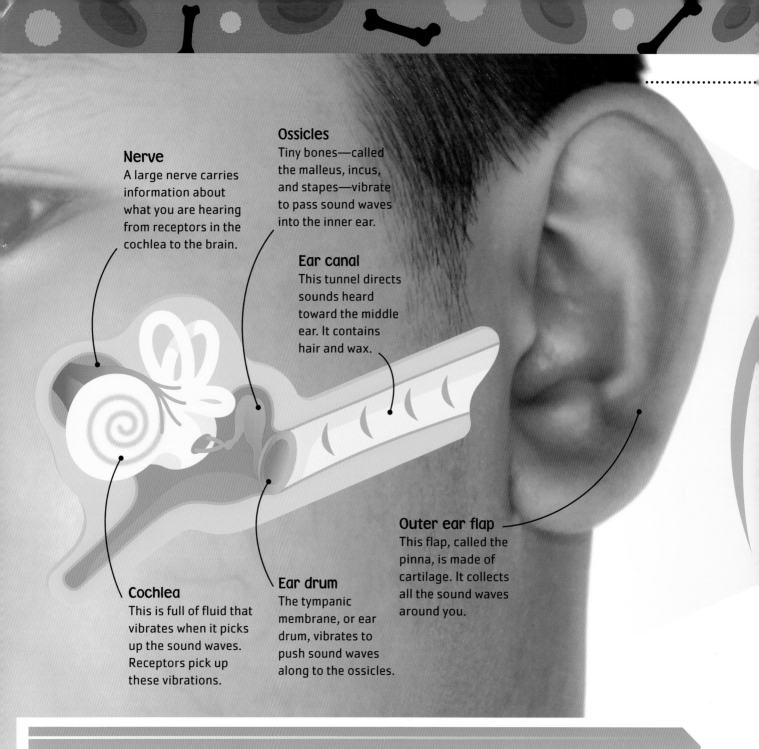

Nerve
A large nerve carries information about what you are hearing from receptors in the cochlea to the brain.

Ossicles
Tiny bones—called the malleus, incus, and stapes—vibrate to pass sound waves into the inner ear.

Ear canal
This tunnel directs sounds heard toward the middle ear. It contains hair and wax.

Cochlea
This is full of fluid that vibrates when it picks up the sound waves. Receptors pick up these vibrations.

Ear drum
The tympanic membrane, or ear drum, vibrates to push sound waves along to the ossicles.

Outer ear flap
This flap, called the pinna, is made of cartilage. It collects all the sound waves around you.

Ears and hearing

Your ears don't just help you **hear**, they also help you **balance**. Ears have three parts. The **outer ear** is the part you can see, but ears are much bigger than that—inside your head are the **middle ear** and the **inner ear**.

Hearing sounds

Sound waves travel through the air as vibrations. They are picked up by the outer ear and pass through the middle ear, into the inner ear. Here, a nerve sends the vibrations to the brain as electrical signals. The brain then figures out the sounds that are being heard.

Hearing aids

A hearing aid is a device that can help you to hear better. It makes sounds louder and clearer. Early hearing aids looked like trumpets, but some are now so small that you can hardly see them.

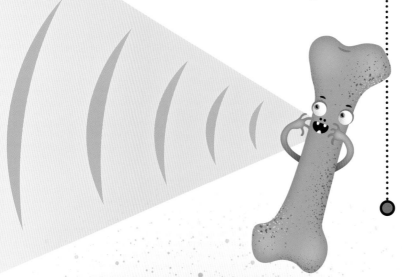

Your ear contains the **smallest bone** in your body—the stapes (stirrup).

EAR WAX

Ear wax is normal and healthy! Made by glands in the ear canal, it traps any dust and dirt, and carries it out of the ear. This protects your ears from infections. Ear wax comes out on its own, so you shouldn't try to remove it yourself.

SPINNING AROUND

FEELING DIZZY

Semicircular tubes inside your ears contain fluid to help you balance. The fluid moves when your body moves, so your brain is aware of your body's position. If you spin around and then stop, the fluid continues to move around for a while, so the brain gets confused and you feel dizzy!

Taste and smell

These senses are **linked together**. You can't taste how tasty food is unless you can also smell it. Your senses of taste and smell can also **keep you safe**—for example, by warning you when food has gone bad.

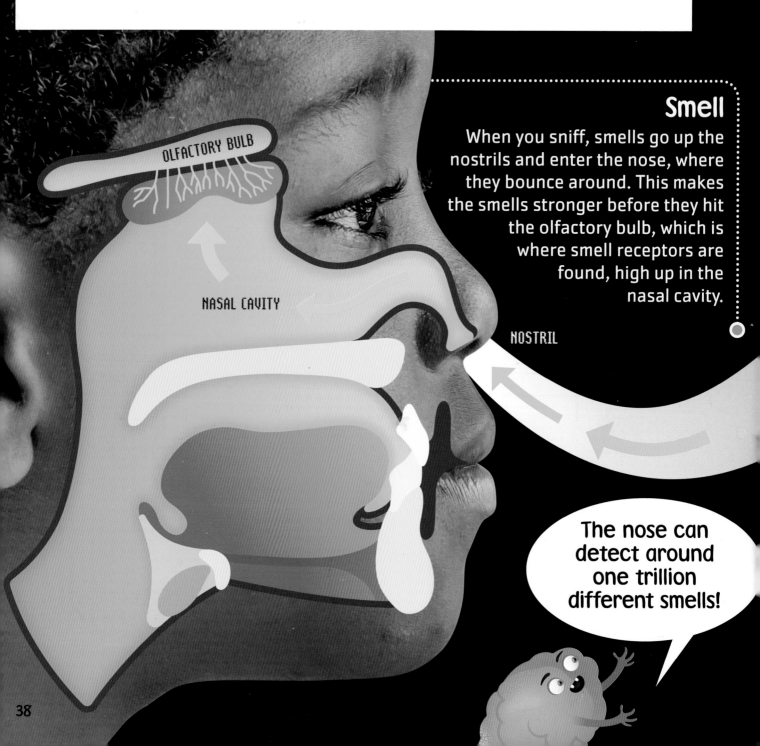

OLFACTORY BULB

NASAL CAVITY

NOSTRIL

Smell

When you sniff, smells go up the nostrils and enter the nose, where they bounce around. This makes the smells stronger before they hit the olfactory bulb, which is where smell receptors are found, high up in the nasal cavity.

The nose can detect around one trillion different smells!

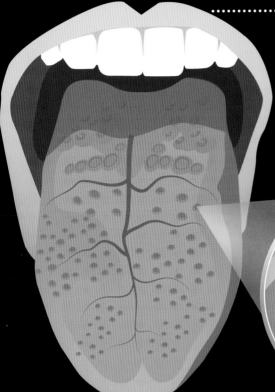

Taste

The tongue has a lot of little bumps on its surface called papillae, which have taste buds on them. Eight tongue muscles help move food around in your mouth, and bring it in contact with the taste buds.

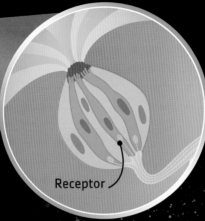

Receptor

Taste buds

Taste receptors found inside the taste buds send information back to the brain so that it can figure out what you are tasting.

Sniffing brings more **smell particles** into the nose!

Types of taste

We can smell countless different smells, but we can only taste five basic flavors. These are sweet, sour, salty, bitter, and umami (savory).

Sweet

Sour

Salty

Bitter

Umami

Teeth

The main job of **teeth** is to break down the food you eat. **Saliva** (spit) produced in your mouth kills bacteria and helps keep your teeth healthy. Everyone has **two sets of teeth** in their life: first baby teeth and then adult teeth.

Brushing your teeth twice a day helps keep them healthy!

Different jobs

There are four types of teeth—each is shaped differently since they all have a different job to do. See if you can notice the straight, pointy, and flat teeth in your mouth.

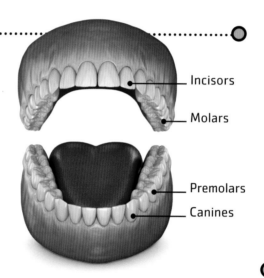

Incisors

Molars

Premolars

Canines

Inside a tooth

The part of the tooth you can see is called the crown. The part hidden inside the gums is called the root. Each tooth is filled with nerves and blood vessels that keep it healthy.

Incisors
These straight-edged teeth at the front of the mouth help you bite food and cut it into pieces.

Canines
Canines are really pointy and sharp. They grip and pierce food, and tear it into smaller shreds.

Enamel is the hardest substance in the body and protects the crown of the tooth.

Dentin makes up most of the tooth and is very hard.

Gums surround each tooth and protect the delicate roots.

Pulp contains a lot of blood vessels and nerves. The nerves allow you to feel pain in your teeth.

Teeth are held in the skull by the jawbones.

BABY TEETH

A baby's first teeth, called milk teeth, begin to grow at around six months old. A child has a full set of 20 milk teeth by the time they are three years old. These start to fall out around the age of six, and are replaced with 32 adult teeth.

Premolars

Smaller than the molars, these teeth help to crush food down further.

Molars

These big and chunky teeth help to grind food into mush that is small enough to swallow.

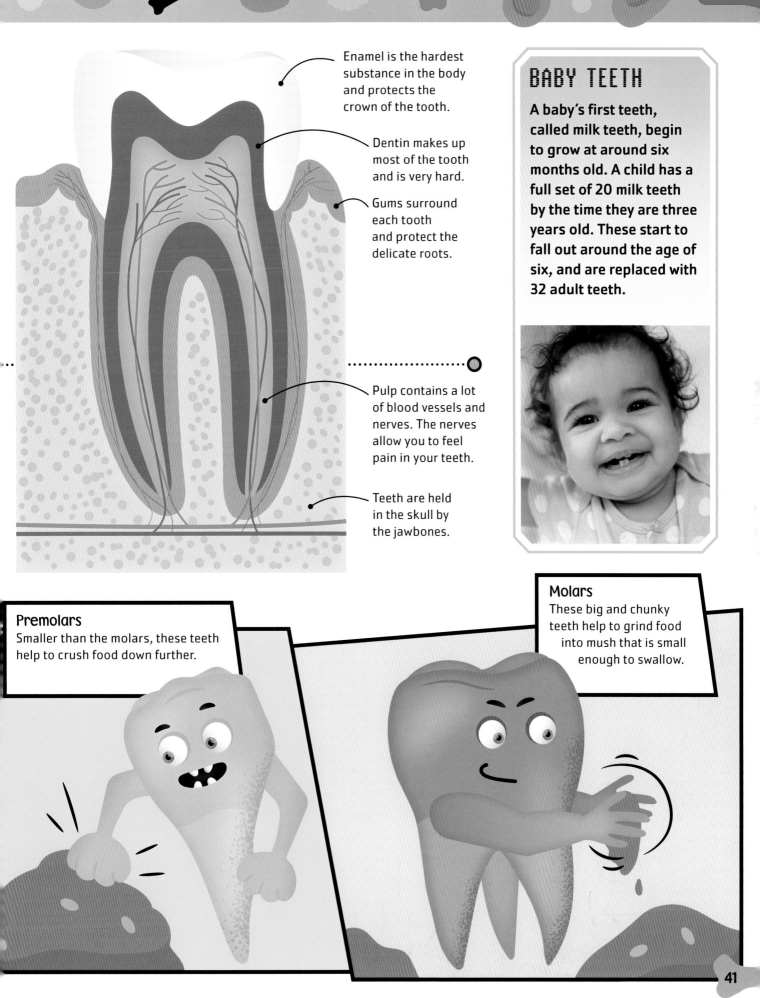

The journey of food

Food contains nutrients, which **give us energy** and **repair broken cells**. When you eat, your food is broken down so that the **nutrients can be absorbed** into your blood and used by the body. This is called **digestion**.

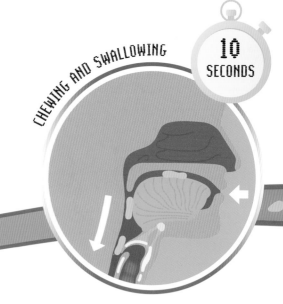

10 SECONDS

When you chew, your teeth cut food into smaller pieces. The food is mixed with saliva, or spit, which contains chemicals that break the pieces down further. It is then swallowed and moves down the esophagus to the stomach.

Digesting food

Food is digested in a very long tube that starts at your mouth and ends at your anus. It can take from one to three days for a meal to pass through the digestive system.

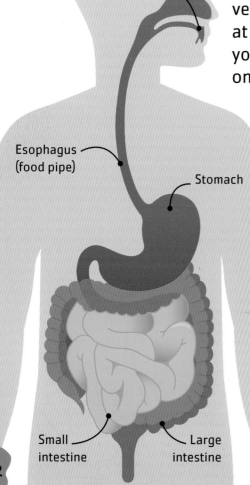

Mouth

Esophagus (food pipe)

Stomach

Small intestine

Large intestine

Some food, like sweet corn, is hard to digest and might come out whole in your poop!

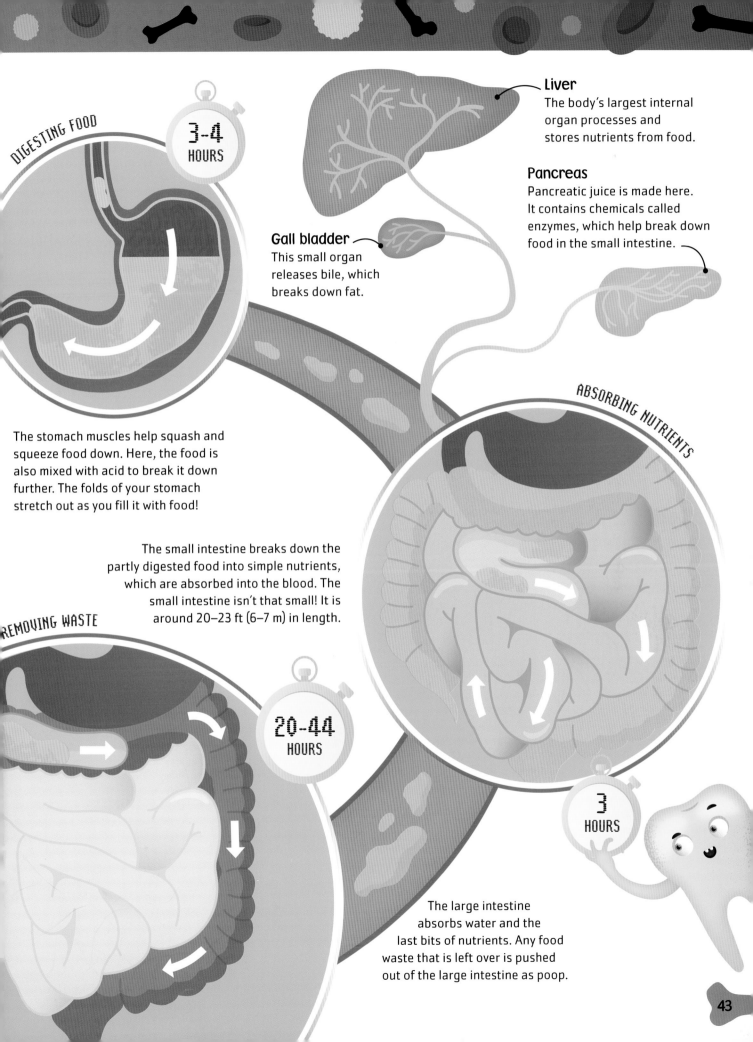

DIGESTING FOOD

3-4 HOURS

Liver
The body's largest internal organ processes and stores nutrients from food.

Pancreas
Pancreatic juice is made here. It contains chemicals called enzymes, which help break down food in the small intestine.

Gall bladder
This small organ releases bile, which breaks down fat.

The stomach muscles help squash and squeeze food down. Here, the food is also mixed with acid to break it down further. The folds of your stomach stretch out as you fill it with food!

ABSORBING NUTRIENTS

The small intestine breaks down the partly digested food into simple nutrients, which are absorbed into the blood. The small intestine isn't that small! It is around 20–23 ft (6–7 m) in length.

REMOVING WASTE

20-44 HOURS

3 HOURS

The large intestine absorbs water and the last bits of nutrients. Any food waste that is left over is pushed out of the large intestine as poop.

Kidneys

The kidneys do a lot of important jobs. They filter around 4 fl. oz (120 ml) of blood every minute. They also help control blood pressure and produce a hormone—a chemical messenger—to make new red blood cells.

NEPHRON

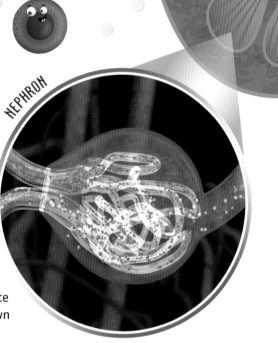

Removing waste

Each kidney has millions of tiny filtering units called nephrons. As the blood passes through these tubes, waste products are separated, and trickle down a tube called the ureter to the bladder.

URETER

BLADDE

Cleaning the blood

Most people have two **kidneys** that filter blood to keep it clean. Waste substances and extra water the body doesn't need are removed and stored in the **bladder**. These then leave the body as **urine**.

URETHRA

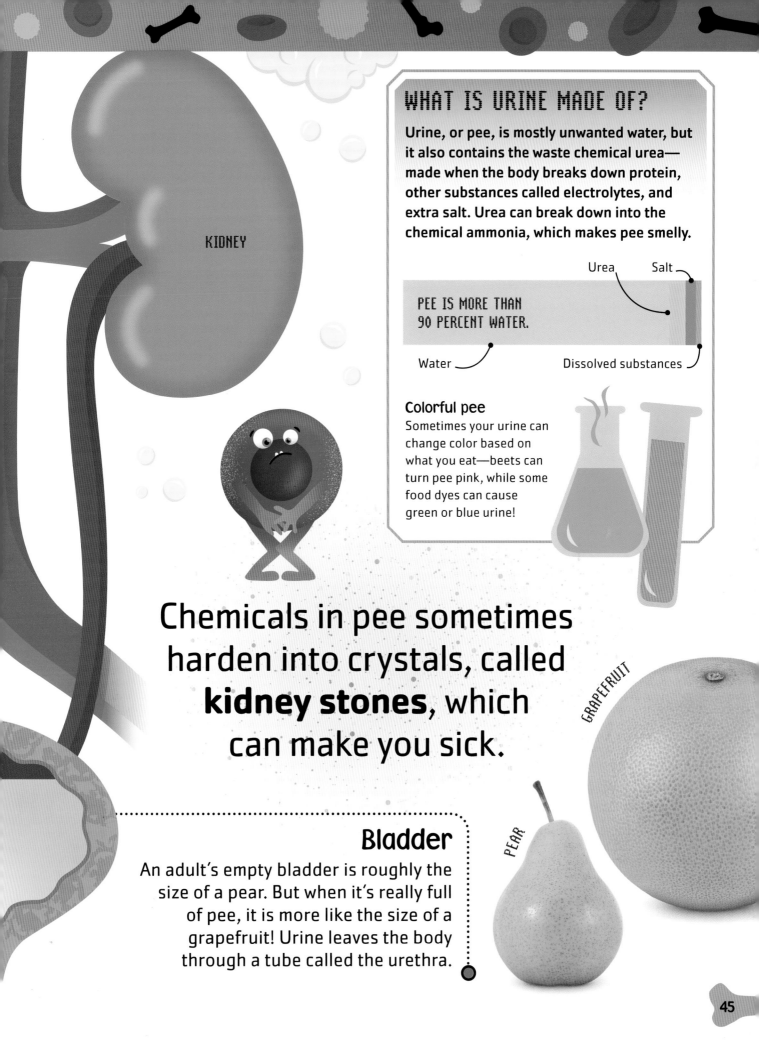

KIDNEY

WHAT IS URINE MADE OF?

Urine, or pee, is mostly unwanted water, but it also contains the waste chemical urea—made when the body breaks down protein, other substances called electrolytes, and extra salt. Urea can break down into the chemical ammonia, which makes pee smelly.

Urea   Salt

PEE IS MORE THAN 90 PERCENT WATER.

Water   Dissolved substances

Colorful pee

Sometimes your urine can change color based on what you eat—beets can turn pee pink, while some food dyes can cause green or blue urine!

Chemicals in pee sometimes harden into crystals, called **kidney stones**, which can make you sick.

GRAPEFRUIT

Bladder

An adult's empty bladder is roughly the size of a pear. But when it's really full of pee, it is more like the size of a grapefruit! Urine leaves the body through a tube called the urethra.

PEAR

The story of medicine

The way **doctors** and **scientists** think about the body has changed over **thousands of years**. Modern medicine began with discoveries made centuries ago, but new **treatments** are being found all the time.

Surgical tools
This carving from around 100 BCE shows us that the ancient Egyptians used basic tools like scalpels (sharp blades) and forceps for small operations.

Ancient medicine
Thousands of years ago, willow bark was found to relieve pain. It contains a similar chemical to aspirin. It was used in ancient China, Egypt, Greece, and Sumer.

You can see me in X-rays!

X-rays
German scientist Wilhelm Röntgen took the first X-ray in 1895. He asked his wife to place her hand in front of the X-ray machine and made a picture of her bones.

Germ theory
Until the 19th century, it was not known that germs caused disease. Ignaz Semmelweis, a Hungarian doctor, discovered that hand washing reduced the spread of infections.

Penicillin
In 1929, Alexander Fleming, a Scottish scientist, found that certain molds stopped bacteria from growing. This discovery led to the first antibiotic, penicillin, being made in the 1940s.

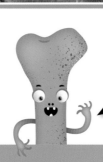

The mold *Penicillium* naturally kills bacteria.

DNA
The structure of DNA was figured out by British scientists James Watson and Francis Crick in 1953. This finding was hugely important in understanding how the body functions.

This artificial toe from an Egyptian mummy is around 3,000 years old.

Amputations

If a limb becomes too badly injured, it is removed, or amputated. Artificial replacements for missing limbs were first made by ancient civilizations.

Herbs were originally used to reduce pain, but they weren't very effective!

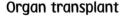
MODEL OF AN ETHER INHALER

Star charts

In the 14th century, European doctors checked the positions of the stars before treating patients. They believed the planets, the moon, and star signs affected the body.

Barber surgeons

In medieval Europe, barbers, who usually cut hair, also performed minor surgeries, such as tooth extraction. They displayed striped poles outside their shops.

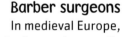

Anesthetic

In the 1840s, a pain-killing medicine, or anesthetic, called ether became popular for use during surgery. It helped ease the pain of operations.

John Hunter

British surgeon John Hunter, born in 1728, had a scientific approach to the human body. He collected and displayed specimens of animals and humans for everyone to learn from.

Organ transplant

The first organ transplant took place in the United States in 1954, when a kidney was transferred from one person to another.

Robotic surgery

Robots are now used to carry out some surgeries. The robot arms are controlled by a human surgeon through a computer.

The human life cycle

As we get older, we go through **different stages** in life. Our **bodies change** and we look different. The way we think also changes based on our **experiences**. It's all part of the human life cycle.

Everyone starts life as an embryo. An embryo forms when an egg cell and a sperm cell join in a process called conception.

The embryo grows quickly and by eight weeks, it looks like a tiny person with arms, legs, eyes, and a nose. It is now called a fetus.

Newborn babies need feeding, cleaning, and cuddles since they can't do anything for themselves. They cry to communicate if they are hungry or tired.

Toddlers are curious about the world around them. They start to explore their surroundings and try to walk. They also make sounds and begin to form words.

Embryo

Fetus

Baby

Toddler

BABY IN THE UTERUS

Pregnancy

A baby starts off as a small ball of cells in its mother's uterus, which multiply quickly to form a fetus. A tube attached to the baby's belly button delivers all the food and nutrients it needs to help it grow. After around forty weeks, the baby is ready to be born.

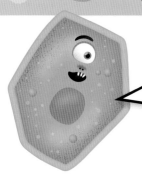

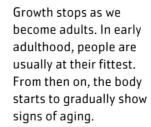

Puberty is when the body becomes more adult-like.

Children make friends, and learn a lot of new things. They need to eat more to support their growing bodies and brains.

Teenagers grow quickly and their bodies change shape. Their behavior and attitudes also change as they learn to be more independent.

Growth stops as we become adults. In early adulthood, people are usually at their fittest. From then on, the body starts to gradually show signs of aging.

In old age, the body loses muscle and bones get weaker. Hair turns gray and the skin wrinkles. Most people live for more than seventy years.

Child

Teenager

Adult

Older adult

BODY CHANGES

Strong bones
When babies are born their bones are soft. These harden by the age of four.

Hair growth
During puberty, people get more body hair, especially in the armpits and groin.

Shrinking body
As people age, the disks in the spine lose water, making the spine shorter.

49

A balanced diet

Your body turns the food you eat into energy. There are five main food groups, and you need to eat a different amount of food from each of them in order to stay healthy.

Carbohydrates

Carbohydrates are found in foods such as potatoes, pasta, bread, and rice. They are the body's main source of energy.

Fruit and vegetables

These foods contain many vitamins and minerals, which help your body fight infections. Different colored fruit and vegetables have different benefits.

Keeping
healthy

Your body needs **energy** to keep it working well. The **foods you eat** and how much you **move your body** can affect your energy levels throughout the day.

Daily exercise

There are so many benefits to exercise and keeping active. It not only helps to keep the body fit and strong, but also keeps your mind healthy and makes you feel good.

Bones and muscles

Exercise makes your body work harder, and helps your bones and muscles get stronger.

Burn calories

Exercise helps you use up extra calories your body doesn't need.

Your body is two-thirds water! That's why you should drink a lot of water every day.

Protein

Protein builds muscles and repairs cells. Meat, fish, eggs, beans, and lentils are good sources of protein. Some protein-rich foods, like oily fish, also help keep the heart healthy.

Dairy

Milk, cheese, and yogurt contain calcium, which makes bones and teeth strong. Dairy foods like these also contain protein and give you energy.

Fat

A small amount of fat is good for you. Sources of healthy fats include olive oil, avocados, nuts, and seeds.

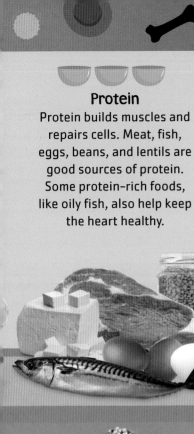

Feel good

Your brain releases chemicals that make you feel good.

More energy

Your lungs and heart work harder, delivering more oxygen to the body.

Socializing

Exercise is a good way to have fun and spend time with friends.

Better concentration

Increased blood flow to the brain makes you more alert and awake.

Improved sleep

Exercising during the day can help you get a better night's sleep.

Sleep

When you are asleep, your body has a chance to **rest** and your brain can **sort** through information collected from the day's events. Most people spend **one-third** of their lives sleeping!

Benefits of sleep

It is important to get enough sleep each night to keep you healthy. Without it, you become tired and irritable. Your body starts to slow down and you are more likely to get sick.

Growth
During sleep, your body releases a growth hormone.

Memory
Your brain logs the day's important information in your memory.

Mood
Good quality sleep lifts your mood.

Healing
Your body repairs and renews cells when you are asleep.

Energy
After a restful sleep, you wake up with more energy.

Sleep patterns

There are different stages of sleep, split into REM (rapid eye movement) and non-REM sleep. You cycle through these stages a number of times during the night. Sleep starts off deep and gets lighter as the night progresses.

Awake	
REM	During REM sleep, your eyes move very quickly under your eyelids. This is when dreams take place.
Light	You move around a lot more and are easier to wake during light sleep than in deep sleep.
Deep	Your body grows and repairs its cells during the deepest stage of sleep.

Try to go to sleep at the same time every day.

Keep your bedroom dark and cool.

Tips for good sleep
When it gets dark, your body realizes it is time to sleep. There are certain things you can do to help you get a good night's rest.

Stop looking at screens two hours before bedtime.

Wear comfortable clothes!

Avoid food and drinks containing caffeine, such as chocolate and carbonated drinks.

An average 6–9 year-old needs
9–12 hours
of sleep a night.

8 P.M. 9 P.M. 10 P.M. 11 P.M. 12 A.M. 1 A.M. 2 A.M. 3 A.M. 4 A.M. 5 A.M. 6 A.M. 7 A.M.

Happy
When something good happens or we do something we enjoy, it makes us feel happy.

Angry
We may feel angry if someone is unkind to us or if we think something is unfair.

Sad
We might feel sad about big changes, such as if a good friend moves away to another city.

Emotions

Emotions are what we feel when we see, do, or hear about something, and they are controlled by the brain. It is normal to feel a lot of different emotions in different situations. Fear, joy, sadness, and anger are all emotions.

Staying healthy

Everyone feels different emotions at times, and there are many things you can do to keep your mind healthy. Poor mental health can have a negative effect on your physical health, too.

Mental **health**

As well as looking after your body, it is important to **take care of your mind** and how you feel. This is called mental health. The state of your mental health affects how you **think**, **feel**, and **act**.

Writing down how you are feeling can be a great help.

Scared

We often feel frightened if we think something bad is about to happen. People get scared by different things.

Excited

Looking forward to something, such as a party or a vacation, can make us feel excited.

Worried

It is common to feel worried when there is a problem we don't know how to handle.

Talking

Sharing your worries with someone else may help you feel better. It also means they can try to support you.

Friends

Spending time with your friends and doing activities together can make you feel happy.

Sleeping

If you don't get enough sleep each night, you might become irritable and find it hard to concentrate.

Hobbies

Doing things you enjoy helps you relax. Hobbies include painting, music, playing sports, and reading.

Exercise

Daily exercise, such as walking, bike riding, and swimming, keeps your mind and body healthy.

Healthy eating

Certain foods, like sugar, can affect how you think, so you should eat a balanced diet with a lot of fruit and vegetables.

Body talk

The way you stand, what expressions you make, and how you position your hands tell others about what you're **thinking** and **feeling**, without you having to say a word!

Disgust
Wrinkling your nose can show you are digusted.

Closed
Crossing your arms in front of your chest shows you might be feeling angry.

Hand gestures

People often use their hands as a way of communicating. Making various shapes with your fingers and thumbs can mean certain things. Be careful though—some signs mean different things in different societies.

Shaking hands can be a friendly way to say hello to someone.

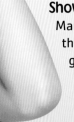

Showing love
Many people around the world make a hand gesture in the shape of a heart to represent love.

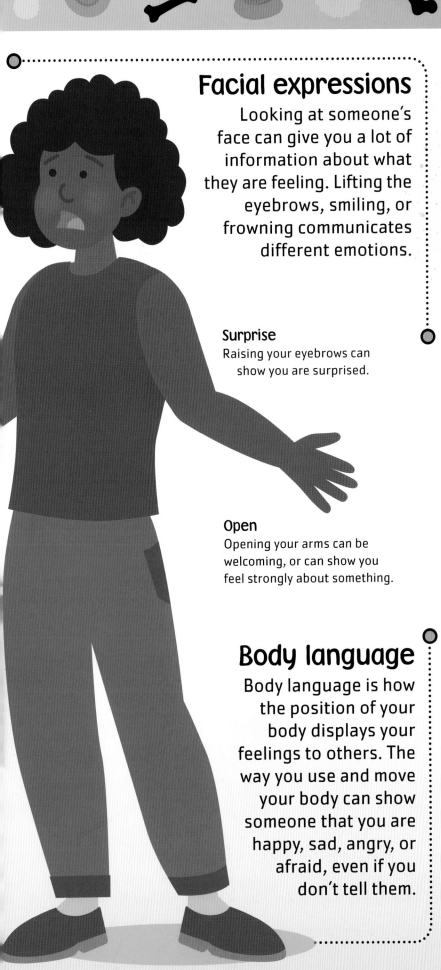

Facial expressions

Looking at someone's face can give you a lot of information about what they are feeling. Lifting the eyebrows, smiling, or frowning communicates different emotions.

Surprise
Raising your eyebrows can show you are surprised.

Open
Opening your arms can be welcoming, or can show you feel strongly about something.

Body language

Body language is how the position of your body displays your feelings to others. The way you use and move your body can show someone that you are happy, sad, angry, or afraid, even if you don't tell them.

A lot of **body language** happens unconsciously.

Slow down!

UNDERWATER SIGNS

Divers exploring the ocean make signs with their hands to communicate with each other. It's impossible for them to speak since they have a tube in their mouth to help them breathe.

This diver is signaling that there is a shark approaching.

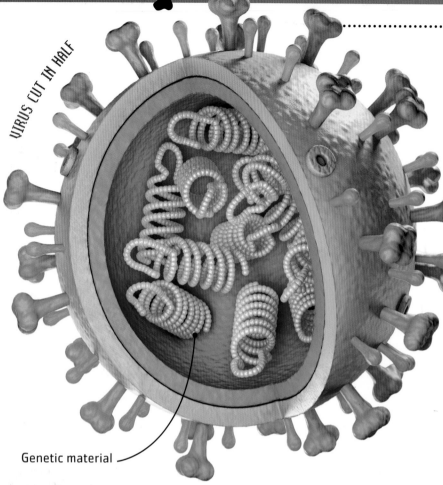

VIRUS CUT IN HALF

Genetic material

Viruses

A virus has proteins on its surface, which allow it to infect a body cell. Once inside, the virus injects its genetic material and takes over the cell. The cell makes many copies of the virus—these are then released to infect other cells.

Surface protein

Hand washing removes bacteria and viruses from your hands!

Viruses and bacteria

Viruses and bacteria are **tiny organisms** that can make us sick. Each bacterium is made up of **one cell** and can live in or on the body. Viruses are **much smaller** and need to get inside the body's cells to be able to survive.

Catching a cold

Many viruses can only survive for a short time outside the body. They need to hop between people as quickly as possible to spread. Here's how a cold travels around!

Bacteria

Bacteria can be good or bad. Many good bacteria live in the body, for example in the intestines, and help to keep it healthy. Bad bacteria, however, can cause infections and may need to be treated with medicine called antibiotics.

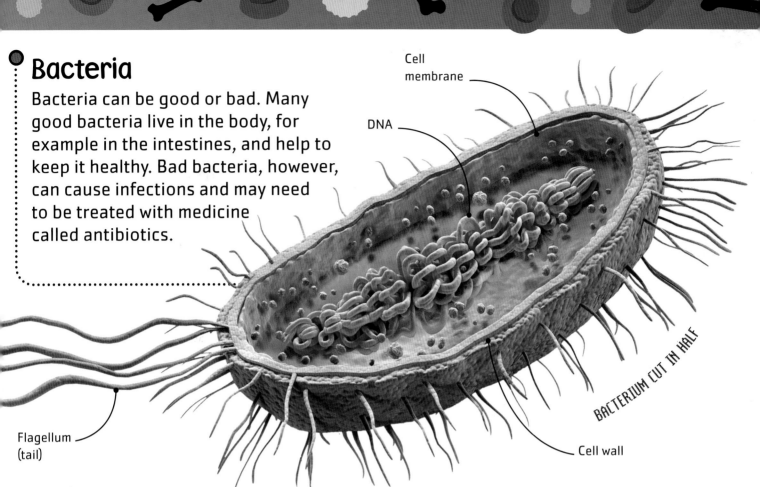

Cell membrane

DNA

BACTERIUM CUT IN HALF

Flagellum (tail)

Cell wall

① A person infected with a cold virus coughs on their hand.

② They shake hands with a friend and pass on the virus.

③ When their friend itches their nose, the virus enters their nostrils.

④ Now infected, the friend transfers the virus onto a handrail.

⑤ Someone else touches the handrail and the virus sticks to their hand.

⑥ When this person eats an apple, the virus gets in their mouth and infects them, too!

≪ VACCINES

A vaccine is an injection that trains the body to kill a virus. Edward Jenner, an English doctor, invented the first vaccine in 1796. It stopped people from catching a deadly virus called smallpox.

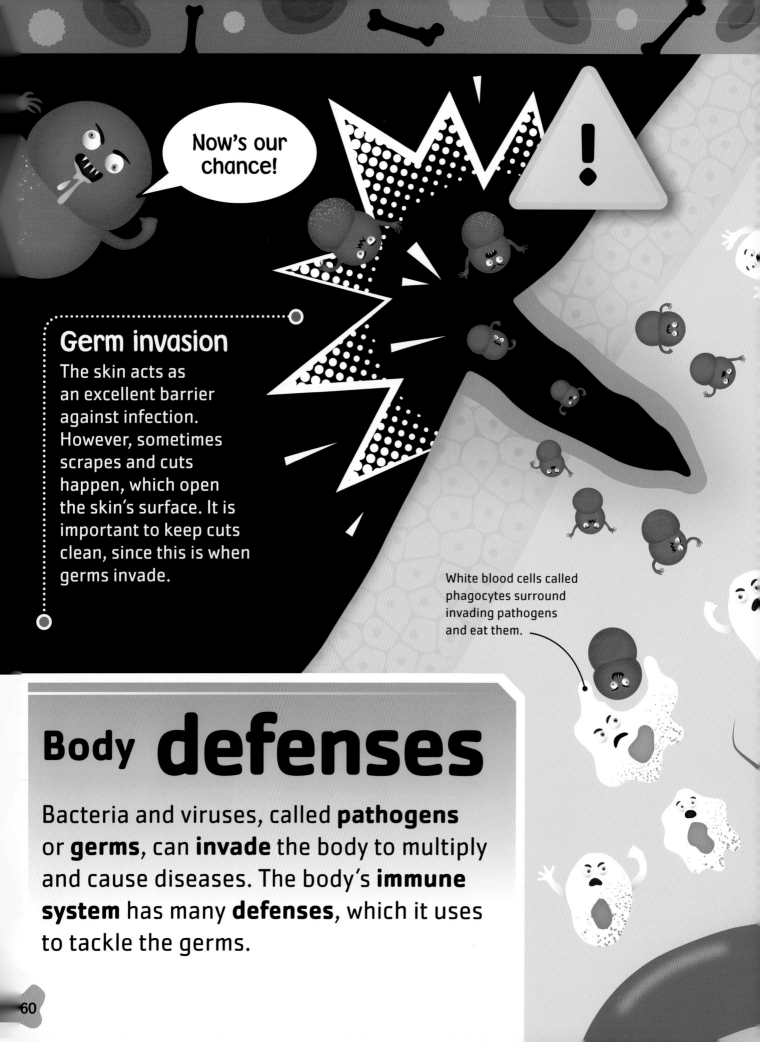

Now's our chance!

Germ invasion

The skin acts as an excellent barrier against infection. However, sometimes scrapes and cuts happen, which open the skin's surface. It is important to keep cuts clean, since this is when germs invade.

White blood cells called phagocytes surround invading pathogens and eat them.

Body defenses

Bacteria and viruses, called **pathogens** or **germs**, can **invade** the body to multiply and cause diseases. The body's **immune system** has many **defenses**, which it uses to tackle the germs.

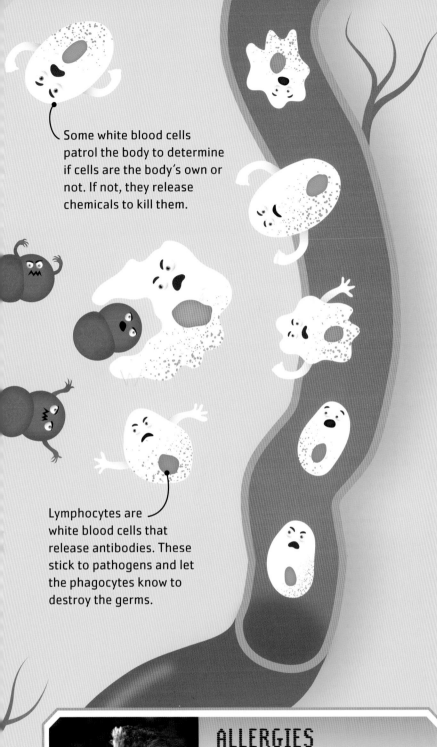

Some white blood cells patrol the body to determine if cells are the body's own or not. If not, they release chemicals to kill them.

Lymphocytes are white blood cells that release antibodies. These stick to pathogens and let the phagocytes know to destroy the germs.

Other defenses

Your immune system is constantly protecting you from pathogens. However, there are other defenses in the body that also help protect against germs.

Hair
Hair acts as a barrier, which some pathogens have difficulty getting past.

Tears
Tears contain antibacterial substances, which kill germs that get into your eyes.

Saliva
It's easy to eat bacteria, but saliva contains chemicals to stop them from multiplying.

Mucus
Slimy mucus can trap pathogens, so they can't invade the body further.

ALLERGIES

The body sometimes reacts to common substances, such as dust or pollen, as if they were pathogens. This causes an allergic reaction. Allergies are usually mild, but sometimes they can be more serious.

Pandemics through time

A pandemic is when a **disease** breaks out all over a **country** or the whole **world**. The disease moves from person to person very quickly to make them ill.

The term "quarantine" comes from an Italian phrase that means "forty days."

EMPEROR JUSTINIAN

The Justinian Plague
Around 540 CE a disease called plague spread quickly around the Mediterranean, killing around fifty million people. This pandemic was named after the emperor Justinian I, who became infected.

Quarantine
The practice of quarantining began in the 1300s, in an effort to stop the plague from spreading. Ships arriving in ports from infected places had to stay for 40 days before anyone could get off.

A red ribbon is worn to show support for those with HIV and AIDS.

HIV/AIDS
Named in 1986, HIV is a virus that spreads via blood and some other bodily fluids. It can lead to a condition called AIDS, which weakens the immune system, but there are now effective medicines to prevent HIV from becoming AIDS.

Air travel
Traveling on airplanes has become more common over the last century, which has allowed diseases to spread faster.

FLEA

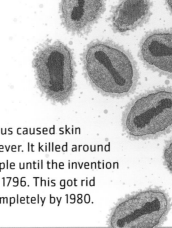

The Black Death
The plague struck again, more than once—first, in the 1340s, killing 200 million people. It was spread by biting fleas. The plague kept returning over the next 300 years and killed most people who caught it. Doctors wore special masks that they thought would protect them.

Smallpox
This deadly virus caused skin rashes and a fever. It killed around 56 million people until the invention of a vaccine in 1796. This got rid of the virus completely by 1980.

Spanish Flu
Spanish Flu spread just after World War I ended in 1918. It was a global pandemic, which killed between 40–50 million people. Despite its name, the disease didn't start in Spain.

Cholera
Cholera is a disease caused by bacteria found in dirty water. A series of pandemics caused by cholera have swept the world from the early 19th century to today.

In the 1860s, a kit that could test water for cholera was invented.

These patients are in a Spanish Flu ward in France during World War I.

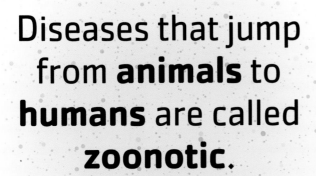

Diseases that jump from **animals** to **humans** are called **zoonotic.**

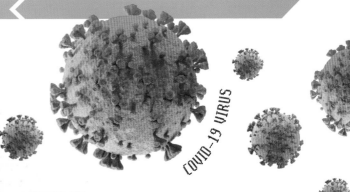

COVID-19
This virus was discovered in 2019. Scientists think it originally came from animals. The virus spreads through droplets of saliva in the air and is now found all over the world.

Medicines

These can be liquids, creams, patches, or tablets that kill germs and repair the body. Some medicines help to reduce pain. Only take medicine following a doctor's instructions.

Pharmacist

Pharmacists know about medicines and can give you advice if you are unwell. They also check what the doctor has ordered and give you the medicine to take home.

Surgeon

Specially trained doctors can open up the body to look inside it and conduct repairs.

Getting
better

When we are sick or injured, we often **need help** to make us feel better. **Health care professionals** are people who can help us, and a number of **treatments** can be used to make us well again.

Diagnosis

People often go to the doctor to get a diagnosis—figuring out what is wrong. They may examine you, advise you to take medicine, or send you to have more tests.

Doctor

A doctor may listen to your chest to check your breathing and measure your temperature to find out what the problem is.

Scanners

Special machines called scanners can take detailed photographs of organs and bones inside the body.

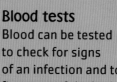

Blood tests

Blood can be tested to check for signs of an infection and to figure out if the body's organs are healthy.

Surgery

Surgery may be performed to repair broken bones and tissues, or remove body parts that don't work well. A medicine, called an anesthetic, is used to put a patient to sleep so they don't feel a thing!

Going to the hospital

People go to the hospital for a number of reasons. An accident that needs urgent attention can be treated at the hospital, and people with chronic (long-term) illnesses may need to go in for regular treatment.

Physical therapist

These people can help you recover after an injury by giving you exercises to do to make your muscles strong again.

Herbal remedies

Early humans used plants and herbs to treat illnesses. Many herbal remedies are still popular today.

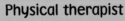

Alternative therapies

Some people use non-medical treatments, such as acupuncture, to help them get better. These are sometimes used alongside herbal remedies.

Acupuncture

Fine needles are placed around the body in acupuncture. This releases substances in the body that can reduce pain.

65

Future bodies

Technology has changed the way we live, gather information, and how our health care systems work. Combining technology and medicine could help us to live **healthier** and **longer** lives.

Personalized medicine

Scientists can now study a person's DNA to make medicines just for them, and this may become much more common. DNA can also reveal if someone is more at risk of certain illnesses.

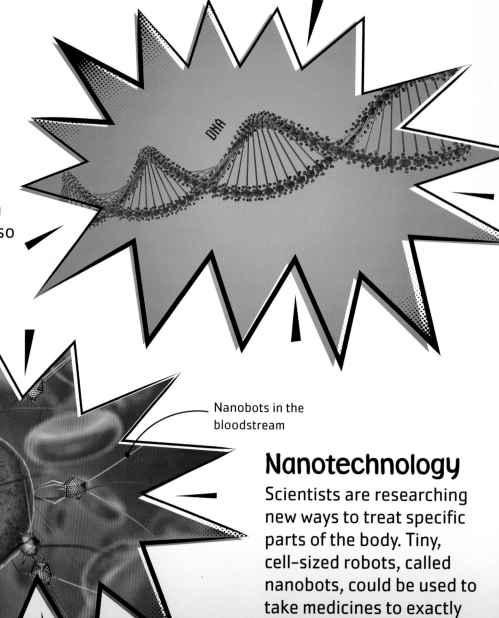

DNA

Nanobots in the bloodstream

Nanotechnology

Scientists are researching new ways to treat specific parts of the body. Tiny, cell-sized robots, called nanobots, could be used to take medicines to exactly where they are needed inside the body.

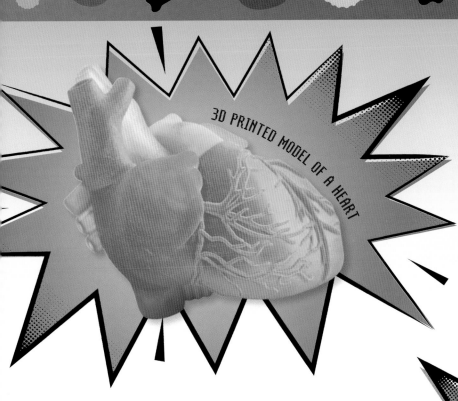

3D PRINTED MODEL OF A HEART

3D printing

In 3D printing, objects are "printed" in layers. Scientists are experimenting with printing plastic models of organs, and then growing cells from a person on the model to make them a new organ!

This is what a bionic eye might look like. The word "bionic" is a combination of "biology" and "electronic."

Bionic body

In the future, we might be able to replace body parts with electronic parts that have extra features. For example, a bionic eye might be able to see much better in the dark than a human eye.

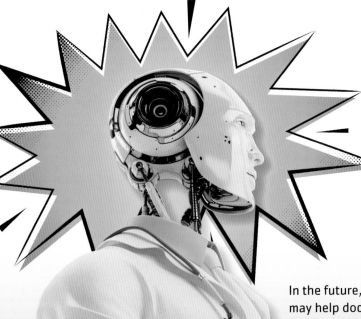

Artificial intelligence

Work is being done to see if computers can read X-rays as well as humans can. If computers can be trained to understand scans, the process of diagnosing patients will become much quicker.

In the future, robots may help doctors diagnose diseases.

Glossary

These words are helpful to know when talking and learning about the body.

anesthetic
medicine used before procedures and surgeries to cause sleep or a numbing feeling, so that pain is not felt

antibiotic
medicine for treating infections caused by bacteria

antibody
special protein created by the blood to attack germs that have infected the body

aorta
largest artery, which carries oxygen-rich blood from the left side of the heart to other parts of the body

artery
blood vessel that takes blood away from the heart to other parts of the body

artificial intelligence
the use of machines to recreate processes and tasks done by humans

bacteria
tiny organisms made up of one cell. Good bacteria help keep the body healthy, while bad bacteria, or bacteria that get in the wrong place, can make a person sick

bile
fluid made by the liver and stored in the gall bladder to help with digestion

blood clot
collection of blood in one place that turns into a partially solid, gel-like state and forms a clump

blood vessel
tube through which blood travels

bone marrow
jelly-like substance found in the center of most bones. Red marrow makes blood cells, and yellow marrow stores fat, which gives you energy

calorie
unit of energy

capillary
smallest type of blood vessel that connects arteries to veins

carbon dioxide
waste gas produced by the body and removed when a person breathes out

cell
basic building block that makes up all living things

chromosome
thread-like structure made up of DNA, found in the nucleus of a cell

contract
become smaller or shorter

dermis
thick inner layer of the skin, which contains nerves, glands, blood vessels, and hair follicles

diagnosis
identification of an illness or disease by looking at symptoms, examining a person, and carrying out medical tests

DNA
short for deoxyribonucleic acid, the chemical that makes up genes

enzyme
special substance created by the body to help speed up processes, for example to break down food in the digestion process

epidermis
thin outer layer of the skin

genes
instructions that build and run the body. Genes are made up of DNA and are found in the chromosomes in a cell's nucleus

gland
organ that makes a substance, such as sweat, hormones, tears, or saliva

hormone
chemical made by a gland and released into the bloodstream, which sends a message to another part of the body

lobe
rounded part of an organ, for example the brain has four main lobes: occipital, frontal, parietal, and temporal

mucus
sticky, protective substance found in different parts of the body, such as the nose, throat, lungs, and stomach

neuron
nerve cell that sends and receives electrical signals to pass messages through the nervous system

nucleus
part of a cell that contains its genetic material and controls its activities

nutrient
substance in food that is needed by the body for energy and growth, and to repair cells

organ
group of two or more tissues that work together to do a job, such as the heart, eye, or brain

organelle
structure within a cell that does a specific job, such as the nucleus

organism
a living thing, such as a plant, animal, or single-celled life-form

oxygen
gas needed by the body to keep cells alive. In humans, oxygen is breathed into the lungs—from there it goes into the blood

oxygen-poor
without much oxygen

oxygen-rich
with a lot of oxygen

pathogen
organism that causes disease, such as a virus or bacterium

protein
basic structure found in living things. Different proteins carry out different functions in the body

pulmonary artery
artery that carries oxygen-poor blood from the right side of the heart to the lungs

pulmonary vein
vein that carries oxygen-rich blood from the lungs to the left side of the heart

receptor
tiny structure on a cell that picks up sensory information, such as light, heat, or pain, and passes the information on as signals to a nerve

saliva
clear liquid made in the mouth by glands called salivary glands, to help keep the mouth healthy

sensor
organ that picks up sensory information, such as light, sound, or touch

tissue
group of cells that carries out similar jobs

transfusion
process in which blood is transferred from one animal to another. A blood transfusion is often given as a treatment to replace blood that has been lost

transplant
medical procedure in which an unhealthy organ in the body is replaced with a healthy one from another person

uterus
organ that is part of the female reproductive system, where a baby develops before being born

vaccine
medicine, usually given as an injection, that trains the immune system to defend the body against a virus

vein
blood vessel that carries blood to the heart from other parts of the body

vena cava
largest vein in the body, which carries oxygen-poor blood to the heart. The superior vena cava carries blood from the upper body, while the inferior vena cava carries blood from the lower body

virus
small particle that can enter an organism and take over a healthy cell, then multiply to cause an infection

X-ray
high-energy form of light that is used to produce photographic images of bones

Index

Aa

acupuncture 65
aging 29, 49
allergies 61
alveoli 22, 23
anesthetics 47, 65
antibodies 19, 61
antigens 19
aorta 17
arms 14–15
arteries 16, 23
artificial intelligence 67
atria 16, 17

Bb

babies 11, 48
baby teeth 40, 41
bacteria 58–9, 60
balance 36, 37
biceps 14–15
bionic body parts 67
bladder 15, 44, 45
blood 9, 16–21, 23, 25, 44
blood clots 21, 29
blood groups 19, 20
blood tests 64
blood transfusions 20
blood vessels 11, 13, 18, 21, 28, 29, 30, 40, 41
body language 56–7
bones 8, 10, 12–13, 15, 49, 50
Braille 33
brain 10, 24–5, 26, 27, 32, 34, 37, 51, 52
breathing 11, 22–3, 25
bronchi 22
bronchioles 22

Cc

capillaries 23
carbon dioxide 11, 16, 17, 18, 22, 23
cardiac muscles 15
cardiovascular system 11
cartilage 13
cells 7, 8, 9, 58
cerebellum 25
cerebrum 24–5
chromosomes 7
cochlea 36
colds 58–9
cornea 34
coronary arteries 16
COVID-19 63

Dd

defenses 60–1
dentine 41
dermis 28, 32
diagnosis 64, 67
diaphragm 23
diet, balanced 50–1, 55
digestive system 8, 11, 42–3
diseases 62–3
DNA 7, 46, 66
doctors 64

Ee

ears 24, 36–7
eggs 11, 48
electrical signals 9, 26, 37
embryos 48
emotions 24, 54–5
enamel 41
energy 9, 50, 51, 52
enzymes 43

epidermis 28, 32
exercise 50–1, 55
eyes 27, 31, 34–5, 67

Ff

facial expressions 56–7
fat cells 9
feet 29
fetus 48
fingers 32–3
follicles 28, 31
food 42–3, 48

Gg

gall bladder 43
genes 6, 7, 58
germs 46, 60–1
glands 28, 29, 31, 37
gluteus maximus 14
goosebumps 31
growth 48–9, 52
gums 40, 41

Hh

hair 28, 30–1, 49, 61
hand gestures 56
healing 19, 21, 29, 52, 64–5
health care 64–5
healthy lifestyle 50–1
hearing 24, 36–7
heart 11, 15, 16–17, 21, 25, 27
hemoglobin 19
herbal remedies 47, 65
hormones 44
hospitals 65

Ii

immune system 11, 60–1
infections 11, 18, 19, 46, 58–9
inheritance 7
intestines 43
iris 34–5

Acknowledgments

DK would like to thank: Vagisha Pushp and Vishal Ghavri for picture research; Kanika Kalra and Vijay Kandwal for hi-res assistance; Polly Goodman for proofreading; and Helen Peters for the index.

The author would like to dedicate this book to her father and brother: "For your unwavering support."

The publisher would like to thank the following for their kind permission to reproduce their photographs:

(Key: a-above; b-below/bottom; c-center; f-far; l-left; r-right; t-top)

4–5 Getty Images / iStock: Inok (c). **6 Dreamstime.com:** Sam74100 (l). **7 Dreamstime.com:** Noriko Cooper (br). **8 Dreamstime.com:** Jlcalvo (cb). **13 Dreamstime.com:** Puntasit Choksawatdikorn (cla); Puwadol Jaturawutthichai (cra). **15 Dreamstime.com:** Jlcalvo (br). **Science Photo Library:** THOMAS DEERINCK, NCMIR (bc). **16 Alamy Stock Photo:** JACOPIN / BSIP SA (bl). **18–19 Getty Images / iStock:** Rodrusoleg (c). **20 Alamy Stock Photo:** Charles Walker Collection (cra); Science History Images (cl, clb). **Dreamstime.com:** Ezumeimages (bc); Odua (cr). **21 Alamy Stock Photo:** Mir Basar Suhaib (tc). **Dreamstime.com:** Alexey Romanenko / Romanenkoalexey (cl). **22 Dorling Kindersley:** Thackeray Medical Museum (br). **24 Dreamstime.com:** Miroslav Ferkuniak (c); Kenishirotie (cb); Piotr Marcinski (br). **25 Dreamstime.com:** Photographerlondon (tc/Boy Running); Viculia (tc/Eye close). **26–27 Getty Images / iStock:** Alex-mit (c). **28–29 Dreamstime.com:** Szefei (t). **29 123RF.com:** Sergey Goruppa (cla). **Alamy Stock Photo:** Kondor83 (cr). **Dreamstime.com:** Andrii Biletskyi (bc); Photosvit (br); Weedezign (tr). **30–31 Dreamstime.com:** Aaron Amat (c). **31 Dreamstime.com:** Razvan Cornel Constantin (ca). **Getty Images / iStock:** Helivideo (br). **32 Dreamstime.com:** Igor Bukhlin (tr); Flynt (c). **32–33 Dreamstime.com:** Starvarz (b). **33 Dreamstime.com:** Omeerk (clb); Hafiza Samsuddin (tl); Aaron Amat (cla); Akbar Solo (br). **34–35 Dreamstime.com:** Andrey Armyagov (c/Background). **36 Dreamstime.com:** Ragsac19 (l). **37 Alamy Stock Photo:** ALAN OLIVER (bl). **Science Photo Library:** LENNART NILSSON, TT (cra). **38 Dreamstime.com:** Marlene Vicente (l). **39 123RF.com:** utima (cb). **Dreamstime.com:** Tonny Anwar (crb); Boroda (cr); Nikolai Zaiarnyi (br); Marilyn Barbone (bl). **40 Alamy Stock Photo:** Alexandr Mitiuc (c). **41 Dreamstime.com:** Fizkes (cr). **44 Dreamstime.com:** 7active Studio (cr). **45 Dreamstime.com:** Andriy Klepach (br/Pear); Oleksandr Shyripa (br/Grapefruit). **46 Alamy Stock Photo:** William Arthur (cla); Science History Images (clb). **Dreamstime.com:** Kalcutta (cra). **Science Photo Library:** A. BARRINGTON BROWN, © GONVILLE & CAIUS COLLEGE (br). **47 Alamy Stock Photo:** Album / British Library (ca); REUTERS (tl). **Dreamstime.com:** Darryl Brooks (cr); Georgios Kollidas (c). **Getty Images / iStock:** Denes Farkas (br). **Science Photo Library:** Science Photo Library (cl). **48 Dreamstime.com:** Jose Manuel Gelpi Diaz (crb/Baby crawling); Nontapan Nuntasiri (crb/newborn baby); Katerynakon (cl); Magicmine (c). **49 Dreamstime.com:** Kdshutterman (l); Roman Samborskyi (cl); Mimagephotography (cr); Roman Shyshak (r). **50 Dreamstime.com:** Onur Ersin (cla); Viktorfischer (ca); Julián Rovagnati (cra); Nevinates (cla/Raw Potato). **50–51 Dreamstime.com:** Svitlana Ponurkina (b). **51 Dreamstime.com:** Akulamatiau (cra/Butter); Pipa100 (cla/Tofu); Sergii Gnatiuk (cla/Glass jars); Draghicich (ca/Cheese); Viktorfischer (ca/Yoghurt); Photosvit (cr); Monkey Business Images (crb/Schoolboy); Vudhikul Ocharoen (crb/Asian girl); Witold Krasowski / Witoldkr1 (cla/Fish); Dreamstime.com: Chernetskaya (crb/Avocado); Chernetskaya (cra/Avocado). **Getty Images / iStock:** Coprid (ca/Dairy box). **53 Dreamstime.com:** Aurinko (tr); Dimarik16 (cla); Daria Medvedeva (tl); Tomasz Śmigla (tc).

55 Dreamstime.com: Chernetskaya (cr); Lightfieldstudiosprod (cl); Anna Kraynova (bl); Godfer (bc); Sasi Ponchaisang (br); Scott Griessel / Creatista (c). **56 Dreamstime.com:** Tom Wang (bl). **57 Alamy Stock Photo:** Hagai Nativ (br). **58 Dreamstime.com:** Andreus (tl). **59 Alamy Stock Photo:** Science Picture Co (tr); Pictures Now (br). **61 Dreamstime.com:** Deyangeorgiev (crb); Jaroslav Moravcik (bl); Pongmoji (cra); Margoe Edwards (cr); Photowitch (br). **62 Dreamstime.com:** Patrick Guenette (ca); Serhii Suravikin (clb). **63 Dreamstime.com:** Heritage Pictures (tl); Satori13 (clb); Sdecoret (br). **Science Photo Library:** EYE OF SCIENCE (tr). **66 123RF.com:** nobeastsofierce (bl). **Dreamstime.com:** Sur (cr). **67 Dreamstime.com:** Denisismagilov (cr); Ronald L (tl). **Shutterstock.com:** Ociacia (bc)

Cover images: *Front:* **Dreamstime.com:** Sdecoret tr, Tinydevil clb; *Back:* **Dreamstime.com:** Eldoctore crb, Volodymyr Horbovyy tl, Sur cla; **Getty Images / iStock:** Inok tr

All other images © Dorling Kindersley